Hand-dyed
Yarn Craft
Projects

Hand-dyed
Yarn Craft
Projects

Debbie Tomkies

GUILD OF MASTER CRAFTSMAN PUBLICATIONS

First published 2004 by
Guild of Master Craftsman Publications Ltd
166 High Street, Lewes
East Sussex, BN7 1XU

Text © Debbie Tomkies 2004
© in the work GMC Publications Ltd

ISBN 1 86108 314 9

British Cataloguing in Publication Data
A catalogue record of this book is available from the British Library

Publisher: Paul Richardson
Art Director: Ian Smith
Managing Editor: Gerrie Purcell
Commissioning Editor: April McCroskie
Production Manager: Hilary MacCallum
Project Editor: Gill Parris
Designers: Phil and Traci Morash, Fineline Studios
Pattern editor: Carol Chambers

Typeface: Myriad

Colour reproduction by Icon Reproduction, London
Printed and bound by Stamford Press in Singapore

Credits
Photographs: Christine Richardson, cover and pp. 6 (right), 7, 52–3, 55–6, 58–9, 61, 63, 66, 68, 71,
73, 75, 77, 80–1, 83, 84, 86, 87, 91, 93, 94, 95, 98, 100, 102 and 104.
US National Oceanic and Atmospheric Administration: p. 10 (top)
All other photographs taken by Peter Tomkies

Black and white illustrations by John Yates, based on sketches by Debbie Tomkies
Colour diagrams by Peter Tomkies

Measurement Notice
Although care has been taken to ensure that the metric measurements are true and accurate,
they are only conversions from imperial; they have been rounded up or down to the nearest
whole millimetre, or to the nearest convenient equivalent in cases where the measurements
themselves are only approximate. When following the projects, use either the imperial or the
metric measurements; do not mix units. (See also the note on measurements on page 149 and
conversion charts on pages 146–150.)

Acknowledgements

This book would not have been possible without:

My husband Pete's patience, support and his lovely
step-by-step photographs

My family's encouragement

My granny teaching me to knit and opening my
eyes to the wonders of hand-made items, created
with love

Friends, especially Julia and Alex, for their
encouragement and willingness to 'destruction-
test' part-completed and finished items, and for
their constructive suggestions.

Thanks to you all!

Contents

Back to Basics

Appendices

Getting Started

Introduction

I have always loved colour, and collect rainbows and rainbow-coloured items as others collect stamps; as anyone who has ever felt the passion of a fiery sunset knows, colour can be a huge influence on our moods and emotions. However, beautiful as it is, colour does have its frustrations: whilst we may 'feel' colours instinctively, all too often when we want to recreate these feelings in our crafts we are hampered by lack of confidence about mixing and combining colours, or hindered by thoughts of complex patterns and difficult techniques.

In this book, therefore, I want to demonstrate how easy it is to produce dramatic results with just some basic techniques, a little understanding of colour and a simple pattern.

Using shop-bought dyes and household equipment I show you how natural, undyed yarns can be transformed by your own customized colour combinations, ranging from the most subtle hues (left), to exotic blends (above). Rainbow dyeing is the main technique used, but spraying, resist, yarn painting and overdyeing are also covered, and you are encouraged to experiment freely with colour.

I then show how your dyed yarn can be made into vibrant, fun accessories. There are six knitted projects and six crocheted projects, and each section starts with very simple shapes – for which you only need to learn one or two stitches to get started – and becomes progressively more complex; however, even the more complicated pieces just require knowledge of a few basic stitches and techniques, all of which are covered in Back to Basics. I then give advice on making up and show how embellishments – such as beads and tassels – can be added to liven up or further personalize your creations, and advice on caring for hand-dyed items.

This is not a book which needs to be read from cover to cover, so feel free to dip in, use the bits you need, and do with them as you will.

Happy designing!

Selecting Yarn for Dyeing

Fig 1.1 Left: cotton; top right: ribbon yarn; bottom right, striped cotton and ribbon

Recommended yarns

I have suggested an appropriate yarn for each project but, if your local yarn supplier does not stock the yarn you need, you can refer to the list of stockists on page 138 for mail order alternatives.

For most of the projects I have chosen natural yarns, which have been scoured (commercially washed) but not otherwise treated, because they take dye very well and usually give reliable results; they also have a feel and drape all of their own which can rarely, in my experience, be matched by a synthetic equivalent.

Fig 1.2 Hand-dyed cotton

Experimenting with alternative yarns

You may wish to change the recommended yarn completely, to mix your own dyed yarns with commercially dyed yarns, or to simply vary your design by inclusion of, for example, a novelty or fashion yarn (see Figs 1.1, 1.2 and 1.3). Experimenting with different textures and fibres is great fun and can give some fantastic results, so be bold and try out your ideas, but bear in mind these basic guidelines:

- Make a few samples before embarking on a large-scale project, in case things don't turn out quite as planned.

- Keep your sample squares and make brief notes on how each square was made: I use a 'yarn record', as shown on pages 142–3. You could photocopy this and use it as the basis for your notes, if you wish.

Fig 1.3 Hand-dyed cotton with stripes of commercially dyed ribbon yarn

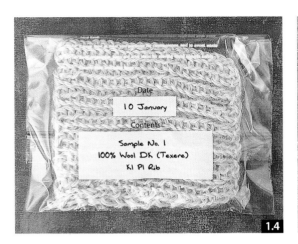

- Cross-reference the record to the swatch by keeping the swatches in clear plastic bags (Fig 1.4), or by attaching a label (Fig 1.5). The resealable bags used for freezer food are ideal, particularly if they have the space for writing details of the contents on the front. The samples, together with your notes, will form a useful record if you want to reproduce a particular technique or style.

How to choose yarn

The composition and structure of a yarn can affect the dyeing process as well as influence the final fabric of a garment or accessory so, whether your choices are made for practical or aesthetic purposes, if the desired effect is to be achieved, the following points must be considered: yarn composition; yarn structure; and whether or not the yarn has been pre-treated.

Yarn composition

Yarn fibres are divided into three main categories: man-made, mixed or natural.

Man-made fibres

With the exception of rayon (see the 'Note' on page 15), man-made fibres are not well suited to home dyeing. This is because the filaments are extremely smooth, and this prevents the dye from penetrating the fibres effectively.

Figs 1.6 and 1.7 Synthetic yarn before and after dyeing

The acrylic yarn in Figs 1.6 and 1.7 on page 13 was dyed in the same bath as the silk in Fig 1.8 (left). The acrylic yarn has taken up very little dye, leaving a patchy, very pale colour, while the silk has produced lovely, varied tones.

Mixed man-made/natural yarns

Yarns with mixed fibres (for example 50:50 wool/acrylic) should take dye, but may produce less satisfactory results than all-natural yarns, particularly where the synthetic content is high. A yarn with a small amount of synthetic content should dye successfully, but always take samples first (Fig 1.9).

Natural yarns

Because synthetics are more difficult to dye, I recommend sticking to natural yarns wherever practical. Natural yarns can be broken down into those made from animal fibres – such as wool, silk, alpaca, angora, cashmere, mohair – (see Fig 1.10) or those which are plant-based – cotton, viscose, hemp, linen – (see Fig 1.11).

Fig 1.9 80/20 viscose (natural)/Lurex (man-made) yarn

Fig 1.10 From left to right: mohair, wool, silk

Fig 1.11 From top to bottom: cotton, hemp, viscose

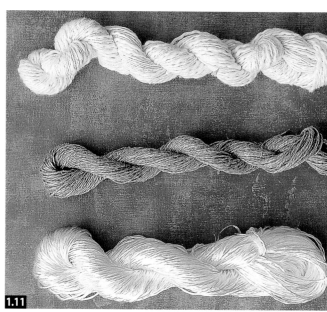

1.12

Animal- (also referred to as protein-) based fibres can be successfully dyed using fibre-reactive dyes and a hot water method (see page 39). Silk, however, can be dyed using either hot or cold water methods (see page 39) – providing the level of heat is kept below 85°C (32°F) – so for silk choose whichever method suits you best.

Plant-based (cellulose) fibres, on the other hand, also work well with fibre-reactive dyes, but using a cold water process.

1.13

Mixed natural fibres

Working with mixtures of exclusively animal fibres or all-plant yarns should not present any difficulties, although the take up of colour may vary depending on the nature of the mix and the fibres used. So, a mix of 80% alpaca with 20% wool could readily be dyed using the hot water method (Fig 1.13). Equally, a cotton/viscose combination could be dyed together using the cold water process (Figs 1.14 and 1.15).

For mixtures of animal and plant fibres, more care is required and both types of fixative (vinegar and sodium carbonate) must be used in the soaking solution. Details of how to fix a mixed-fibre yarn are included in Appendix C (see page 146). Whilst the results of mixed animal/plant fibre dyeing are usually fine, it is perhaps best to stick to all-animal or all-plant combinations initially.

1.14

1.15

Composition and dyeing
In short, yarn composition is very important to the dye process, firstly to establish whether a yarn is likely to take dye well, and secondly to determine the correct dye process to adopt. For best results use natural fibres, the hot water process for animal fibres and the cold water for plant fibres.

Fig 1.16 Smooth, highly twisted, mercerized cotton, undyed (bottom), then dyed at 1%, 2% and 4%

Fig 1.17 Left to right: super-chunky cotton dyed at 4%, 2%, 1% and undyed

As far as the dyeing process is concerned, the structure of a yarn should not, of itself, preclude its use in a particular design. Experiment with the dyebath strength, varying the amount of water left in the yarn, or increasing the level of fixers to achieve your desired results. Do ensure, however, that you sample carefully, keep good records of your samples and bear in mind that the structure of a yarn will have an important impact on the final fabric of the item.

Yarn structure

Here we are interested primarily in the amount of twist in the yarn, i.e. how tightly the yarn is spun; whether it is very smooth or highly textured, and its thickness relative to the amount of twist and texture. Very smooth yarns may take up dye more slowly, particularly if there is also a significant amount of twist in the yarn (Fig 1.16). Thick yarns may also take longer for dye to penetrate and may require a more concentrated dyebath, depending on the amount of twist and the smoothness of the yarn (Fig 1.17).

Yarn treatments

Certain yarns are pre-treated or finished before – or in some cases after – they are spun. Wool and cotton may be bleached to obtain a 'purer' white; cotton may be mercerized for greater strength and lustre; and some wools are also treated to prevent them felting when machine-washed.

While I prefer to use yarns that have been scoured but not otherwise treated, yarns that have been treated will usually still dye successfully, depending on the treatment used; a bleached silk yarn, for example, can

Fig 1.18 From left to right: unbleached, undyed silk; unbleached dyed silk; bleached undyed silk; dyed silk

allow you to produce brighter, more vibrant colours than an equivalent unbleached fibre (Fig 1.18). However, if you do intend to use a treated yarn, sample carefully before committing to a large project.

How do different yarns affect the fabric of a finished article?

Choose a yarn that is appropriate both for the way you want the finished article to look and for the use to which it will be put. For example, a gossamer-fine silk would make a beautiful stole or camisole top, but would be impractical for a duffle-bag or floor cushion. Most of these things are simply common sense but you may find it a useful cross-check to consider the following when choosing your yarn:

Yarn tension

Tension (or gauge) plays a significant part in producing most knitted or crocheted articles. All commercial patterns specify the tension needed in order to produce the item in the correct size and with the correct proportions. Tension is normally checked by making a tension square/swatch, also referred to as a gauge swatch (see Tension/Gauge on page 109). Making and measuring tension squares requires discipline but, even when you are using precisely the same yarn as that specified in the pattern, checking tension is essential.

Checking tension is even more crucial when substituting yarns in a pattern: consider whether you want your finished

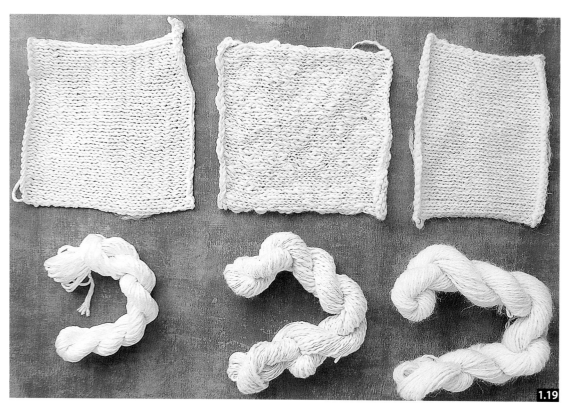

Fig 1.19 From left to right: knitted swatches of silk, cotton, 4ply wool

Fig 1.20 From top to bottom: 4ply wool, cotton, silk

piece to have similar characteristics to the original in terms of size, proportion, drape and handle. If so, use the original yarn as a guide to choosing a substitute yarn; look for one of similar thickness – the fibre content and style of the yarn may be quite different, but the tension should be reasonably similar. A standard 4ply wool yarn, for example, can often be successfully interchanged with a cotton or silk of similar thickness (see Figs. 1.19 and 1.20).

Alternatively, two or more yarns with very similar tensions can be used together to create a wealth of interesting variations (see Fig 1.21).

Fig 1.21 4ply wool and medium-fine silk share similar tension but look very different

What drape/handle do you want?

Once you have found a yarn that knits to the right tension, make sure that the tension square has the right drape and feel for its intended use (see Tension/Gauge, page 109). Is the fabric hard or soft? Is it floppy or stiff? Are there big holes between stitches or are the stitches densely packed together? How easy was it to make your tension square? If, in order to achieve the stated tension you have had to make a significant change in needle size (say, more than three sizes larger or smaller than those stated in the pattern) it may be that your chosen yarn isn't really suitable for your intended project.

Generally, each yarn works best on a small range of needles. With a 4ply yarn, for example, try a needle size in the range US 2 to 5 (2.75mm to 3.75mm/ old UK 12 to 9). For a double knitting yarn, on the other hand, try needles in the range size US 5 to 8 (3.75mm to 5mm/ old UK 9 to 6).

If your needles or crochet hook are too small, the fabric will be hard and unforgiving, too large and the fabric will be very loose and holey. Of course, there will be times when this is desirable – a floaty scarf may benefit from a larger than normal hook to give an airy, light feel. A floor rug may warrant a smaller hook to create a dense, hardwearing fabric.

The same fine knitting needles were used for both swatches in Fig 1.22, and both used a pure cotton yarn. The smaller square on the left has produced a very dense fabric which was stiff to handle, had little give and was hard work to knit. It would make a good floor rug or tote bag, but definitely not a cosy sweater. The larger swatch on the right used a much finer, slubby cotton. It made a lovely lightweight jacket, but would have been entirely unsuitable for anything heavier and wouldn't be very hardwearing. In this case, the fine needles were far better suited to the finer yarn.

1.22

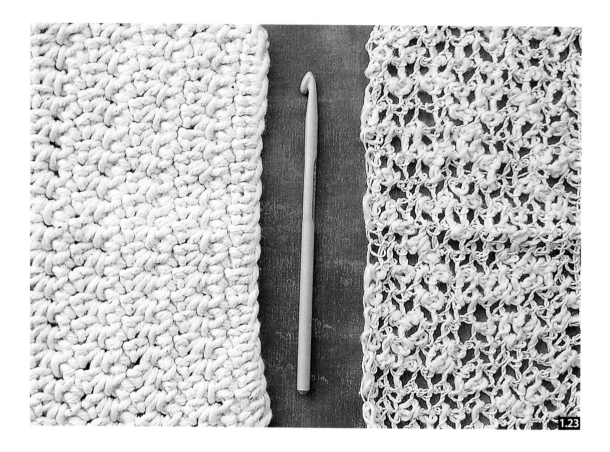

Fig 1.23 (above) shows the same two cotton yarns as used in Fig 1.22 (previous page), this time made using a large crochet hook. The thick cotton yarn is better suited to this hook size, although it still produces a good, compact fabric. The larger hook was more comfortable to work with and didn't feel as if it was going to break, while the finer yarn produced a very flimsy fabric with large holes. On balance, I would only use the large hook with the fine yarn if I was creating something deliberately see-through which wouldn't take much wear, such as a very fine stole or scarf.

What texture are you looking for?

Every yarn has its own texture: smooth, hairy, slubby (yarn with 'lumpy bits') or sleek so, whether you are choosing a yarn to suit your pattern, or vice versa, consider how well the yarn and pattern work together – a very hairy mohair yarn on

Note

Test the tension square
Be guided by your hands and your common sense. Feel the tension square; pull it around a bit, stretch it, scrunch it and hold it up to the light. Don't be frightened to do whatever you think necessary to ensure that it will stand up to whatever use you want from it.

a complex Aran pattern, for example, may not do justice to either the yarn or the pattern. The variations in the thickness and the fluffiness of the yarn may soften the clear lines of the Aran styling, reducing its impact. The same mohair yarn may, however, be perfect when teamed up with a plain stocking stitch or simple crochet pattern as the yarn alone will create sufficient interest without competing with a complex pattern of stitches, as shown in Fig1.24, opposite.

Fig 1.24 Mohair, on left knitted in stocking stitch, and on right knitted with cable pattern. Note how the cable pattern is barely visible, adding little to the attractiveness of the design.

How to care for the yarn?

To avoid heartache in the future, think how you will care for your masterpiece once it is finished. A fine scarf which will receive minimal wear and tear would look beautiful crafted in a delicate cashmere or expensive silk, but the yarn can only be very carefully hand-washed; a rug would need more regular washing with a good detergent, so would be far better suited to a strong cotton or machine-washable chunky wool.

If in any doubt about the suitability of a yarn, make one or more tension squares and wash them at various temperatures, using different detergents if necessary. Check for shrinkage, matting (felting) and bobbling, and make sure that the square returns to the right shape once it is dry. If you don't like hand-washing, make a tension square using undyed yarn and throw it in the washing machine to see if it will cope with a more robust wash. Sometimes, even seemingly delicate yarns will emerge unscathed from a spell in the washing machine. However, if you are in any doubt, don't risk this approach with a finished item. (See also Care of Hand-dyed Pieces, on pages 136–7.)

Colour Schemes for Yarn

What type of dye should I choose?

I have used fibre-reactive dyes throughout this book, because they offer a good choice of colours and can be reliably used on a wide range of fibres using both hot water and cold water methods. They can also be 'fixed' using commonly available ingredients: household salt and white vinegar for animal fibres, and salt and sodium carbonate for plant-based yarns. Fibre-reactive dyes are readily available from most craft suppliers (see page 138 for a selection of stockists).

What colours of dye should I choose?

Your colour choice will depend on personal preference, your budget, and whether you have a specific project in mind. For the projects in this book I suggest limiting yourself to three dyes for a single item. These dyes will form the 'base colours' from which you can produce the various combinations of shades and hues in your finished item.

Three base colours (or less) should allow you to produce additional shades by a combination of blending, dilution, and the addition of black to mute shades if required. If you begin with too many dyes the eventual result may be muddied or over-fussy, as too many colours blend and interblend, each competing for attention in the finished design.

In fact, it is quite possible to produce excellent results with just one dye. A single colour can be used to great effect by simply dividing the stock solution into three or more bottles, diluting each one to a different strength (for example, one at full strength,

2.1

2.2

one with double the volume of water and one with four times the original volume). This dilution of colours – combined with the additional blending achieved during the application of the dyes – can produce a lovely graduated yarn (see Figs. 2.1 and 2.2, facing page). As the shades all derive from a single hue, there are no issues with colour clashing, and with many different shades within the skein the effect can still be really striking.

Choosing your first colour palette

There are a number of methods for selecting good combinations of colours and they are not necessarily mutually exclusive:

Personal favourites

A 'preferred' colour scheme is a good place to start when choosing your first dyes and building up your personal colour palette. My own favourite colours fall within the purple, cerise, blue range, so I keep a good stock of these colours in various shades, wherever possible (see Fig 2.3, above).

What will you be making?

If you want to make clothing or an accessory, pick a couple of your favourite outfits and choose up to three colours from there (see Figs. 2.4 and 2.5, below). For accessories for your home, the best starting point will be the room where you intend to put the finished piece.

2.6

Fig 2.6 (above) shows a selection of items from our living room which I intend to use to form a colour scheme for a floor cushion similar to the one in Project 3 (see page 62).

Start a sourcebook

If you do not have a set colour scheme in mind, or you want to see how a range of colours and/or textures work together, refer to a 'sourcebook'. Details of how to start your own sourcebook and build up your own collection of source materials can be found on page 31.

Rainbow colours

If you want to produce the colours of the rainbow, or to create a wide range of colours from the smallest range of dyes, a basic colour palette of red, yellow and blue would make a great combination (see Fig 2.7, right).

Black and green

If your budget allows, black and green are two further colours which, whilst not essential, are very useful additions to the colour palette; black because it is invaluable for muting or dulling an otherwise 'loud' colour and green because it can be difficult to get a good green from the primaries blue and yellow.

2.7

Colour theory – a basic guide

I cannot hope to do colour theory full justice in this book – try and borrow or buy one of the many excellent books on the subject – but here are the basics, just to get you going.

The colour wheel

The colour wheel is one of the most useful tools in selecting and combining colours for a colour scheme. Most successful colour combinations, whether deliberate or by happy accident, follow a series of rules and these rules can be most readily illustrated and understood by examining the colour wheel. Rules may be there to be broken, but it is helpful to know what those rules are before you can break them successfully and with confidence.

I think the easiest way to understand the colour wheel is to treat it as a rainbow in circular form: the colour wheel runs through the spectrum starting at red, moving clockwise through orange to yellow, to blue via green, from blue on to violet and so back to red. In theory, a colour wheel could have a near-infinite number of segments as each colour can be mixed with its neighbour an unlimited number of times. For our purposes, however, the standard 12-segment (wedge) wheel should be more than adequate (see Fig 2.8, below left).

The wheel starts with the three primary colours (Fig 2.9, below right): red, yellow and blue. These are known as primary colours because they cannot be made by mixing any other combination of colours.

Next, there are the secondary colours (see Fig 2.10): these are created by the mixing of two primaries in equal proportions: so, red plus yellow gives orange, yellow plus blue, green, and blue plus red gives violet.

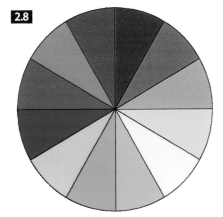

12 segment colour wheel

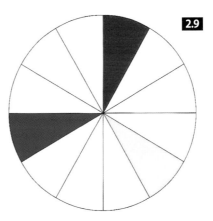

Primaries: red, yellow and blue

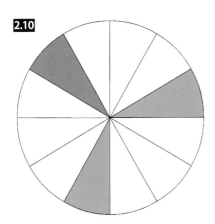

Secondaries: orange, green and violet

2.11

Mixing secondaries:

red + yellow = orange

yellow + blue = green

blue + red = violet

Each of the three secondary colours can be found halfway between the two primary colours from which it is made, as it is an equal blend of its two components (see Figs 2.11 and 2.12, left).

Finally we have the six tertiary colours (Fig 2.13, below left): these are the product of combining a primary colour with its adjacent secondary colour to give red/orange, orange/yellow, yellow/green, green/blue, blue/violet and violet/red (Fig 2.14, below).

Further colours may then be created by mixing neighbouring colours, so:

Blue + Yellow = Green
Green + Yellow = Green/Yellow (Olive green)
Green/Yellow + Green = Dark Olive Green
Or Green/Yellow + Yellow = Yellow Olive Green
And so on …

2.12

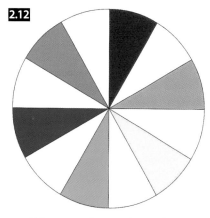

Primary and secondary colours

2.14

Mixing tertiaries:

red + orange = red/orange

orange + yellow = orange/yellow

yellow + green = yellow/green

2.13

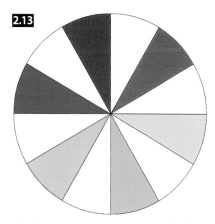

Tertiaries: red/orange, orange/yellow, yellow/green, green/blue, blue/violet, violet/red

green + blue = green/blue

blue + violet = blue/violet

violet + red = violet/red

Of course colours are not always a simple mixture of two or more pure colours. There are three further aspects which influence our chosen colour: hue, value and intensity:

- Hue describes all the colours within the same segment or wedge on the colour wheel. Thus, all the blues in the blue segment are within the blue hue family (Fig 2.15, right) while all the yellows within the yellow segment are part of the yellow hue family (Fig 2.16, below right).

- Value refers to how light or dark a colour is. Within the red segment there will be a range from the deepest burgundy-red to the palest pastel pink. As there is no white dye, colours are lightened by diluting the strength of a pure colour. So, shades of pink result from the dilution of red (see Fig 2.17, bottom right). The more diluted the dye, the paler the colour. Darker shades are obtained by the addition of black dye, but a little black goes a long way, so add it very gradually and do test samples at regular intervals if you are trying to achieve a specific colour.

- Intensity (also referred to as saturation or brightness), describes how bright or dull a colour is. The brightest colour will be the pure colour at the outer edge of its segment in the colour wheel. In dyeing, a colour is dulled by the addition of black or grey (grey being made from a dilution of black dye), or a more subtle effect can be achieved by adding a small amount of a colour's complement from the opposite side of the colour wheel.

So, in practice we may combine two or more pure colours, dilute them to make lighter, paler shades, or add black or a complementary colour to make a duller, more muted shade.

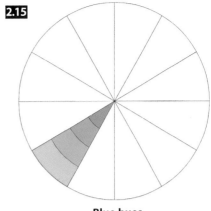

2.15

Blue hues

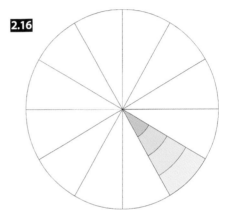

2.16

Yellow hues

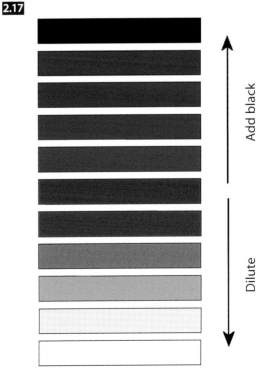

2.17

Add black

Dilute

Values of red

Combining colours:

red + blue = violet

violet + black = dark violet

violet + water = lilac

lilac + black = dusky lilac

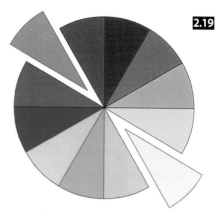

2.19

Complementaries: violet and yellow

2.20

**Violet and yellow in equal proportions
– vibrant and dramatic**

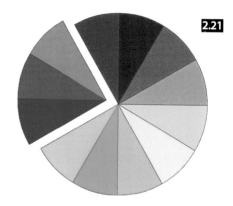

2.21

Harmonies: blue, violet and purple

For example, red plus blue gives violet, which can then be diluted to give a pale violet or lilac shade. Addition of black to the undiluted violet will give a darker, dull purple. When added to the lilac shade, black will produce a soft, dusky lilac (see Fig 2.18, above).

How colours interact in design

Once you have mastered the art of making the colours you want you can, with a little understanding of some basic principles, combine the different colours to achieve a pleasing result.

Complementary (also referred to as contrasting) colours

This term describes two colours on opposite sides of the colour wheel. Thus, blue is the complementary of orange, red of green and violet of yellow (see Fig 2.19, top right).

When two complementary colours are used together, the result is usually dramatic and produces a vibrant effect: the two complementaries enhance and brighten each other (see Fig 2.20, middle right).

Harmonious (or analogous) colours

These colours are found either adjacent or near-adjacent to each other on the colour wheel (see Fig 2.21, above). Harmonious colours share a common colour element in their make-up, so purple is a harmonious colour to blue and violet (purple being blue and violet mixed in equal proportions). Similarly, a mixture of orange and yellow would produce a shade which is harmonious to both yellow and orange.

2.22

Harmonious colours are 'safer' in that they are unlikely to produce colours which clash or which simply don't go together. They need not be boring or unimaginative, but they do tend to be subtler and more restful on the eye. Compare the harmonious red, orange and yellow shades in crisp autumn leaves (see Fig 2.22) with the intense contrast of the vivid pink and yellow in this waterlily (Fig 2.23). Both are equally attractive and both follow the 'rules' of colour theory, but one uses the principles of harmony, the other of complements.

2.23

Colour proportions

The proportion of colours in a design can be as important as combining the 'right' colours, especially when complementary colours are employed. When used in equal proportions, two complementary colours resonate, the one bouncing off the other and making both appear more vibrant.

2.24

2.25

Compare the effect of an equal balance of two complementaries (Fig 2.20 on page 28) with the effect of two very different proportions of colour (Fig 2.24, left), and you can see that where two complementary shades are used in differing proportions the resulting combination will still be lively and vibrant, but the stronger colour will predominate. Note how the tiny amount of orange in the cerise-pink *Osteospermum* in Fig 2.24 really 'lifts' the overall colour scheme. So, if your palette looks a little dull, add a small amount of a complementary to the colour scheme. It can do wonders to liven things up, often without radically changing the overall scheme.

With harmonious colours, on the other hand, the emphasis is more on enhancement than resonance. In an arrangement comprising solely harmonious colours, the effect is likely to be more subtle, with the proportion of each colour serving to alter the balance of the scheme rather than to change it altogether (Fig 2.25, below left).

Use of black

The importance of black for muting and softening colours was mentioned previously. Used alone, however, black can enhance your designs. Although it can be difficult to dye a true black yarn, black can add great drama to a design and narrow stripes of black are very useful for separating colours which might not otherwise be placed adjacently. Black also emphasizes its neighbouring colours, making them stand out, so giving a design more impact.

Putting theory into practice

In the previous chapter I discussed some of the ways in which you might build your starter palette of colours. However, when you want to produce your own colour scheme, a sourcebook (combined with your knowledge of colour theory) comes in very handy.

2.26

2.27

2.28

The new, tiny digital cameras are invaluable here, as you can easily carry one in your bag. They are a little limited but, if you download the images, you need only keep those which are of interest and print them as required.

Photo albums with clear insert pages are useful for storing flat reference material such as magazine pages, postcards, photos, fabric swatches, while boxes are useful for small objects (pretty marbles, beads, ribbons).

If possible, make a quick note of where each piece came from and why you liked it.

Tip

Creating a sourcebook

A sourcebook is really just a collection of pictures and objects which appeal to you and from which you can draw inspiration – shells, bits of driftwood, shards of pottery, seedheads, or whatever you find interesting. The burnished shades in this metal fish sculpture (Fig 2.26, top left) and the small piece of stone with its beautiful colours (Fig 2.27, top right) were the inspiration for the yarn in Fig 2.28, above. This yarn was used to make Project 8, the sleeveless silk top on page 86.

2.29

2.30

Using your sourcebook in your designs

When needing inspiration, arrange pieces from your source collection that fit the mood or style you are trying to create, to see how the different colours and proportions work. Keep changing the pieces until you are happy with the balance of colours (and textures if appropriate), then use your final collage as a basis for your colour scheme; make a careful note of the colours used, the proportion of each colour and the way in which the colours were placed in relation to each other. The combination of items in Fig 2.29 (above) was the inspiration for the skeins in Fig 2.30 (left). These skeins were, in turn, used to make Projects 1 and 2, the scarf and matching tasselled wool hat (see pages 55 and 58).

Take a photograph of your final arrangement and use this as your point of reference for the design. This is particularly useful if you need to reclaim the surface on which they were displayed.

Tip

Basic Dyeing Equipment

3.1

Dyeing need not require extensive or expensive equipment (see Fig 3.1, above). Apart from the basic protective/safety equipment (rubber gloves, overalls or apron, dust mask and newspapers to cover surfaces), you will need:

Buckets

One or more good-sized, plastic or stainless steel buckets to soak yarn before dyeing and to rinse and wash dyed yarn. They also come in handy for carrying wet yarn around. Stainless steel buckets have the added advantage that you can heat yarn in them on the stove top, but they are very expensive compared to plastic.

Dye pots

Unless you plan to fix your yarn using a steamer, you will need a selection of microwaveable and/or ovenproof wide, flat-bottomed dishes, preferably with lids. Choose dishes that are as large as possible, whilst still, of course, fitting inside your microwave/oven. I find the clear glass, ovenproof type best as they double up for both microwave and oven (as well as for cold water) methods. They are also robust, easily cleaned and you can see the yarn inside. Always clean thoroughly after each dye session.

For oven and hob methods, stainless steel, enamel or the hob-type heatproof glass pans will be fine, but not iron or aluminium which can react with the dyes.

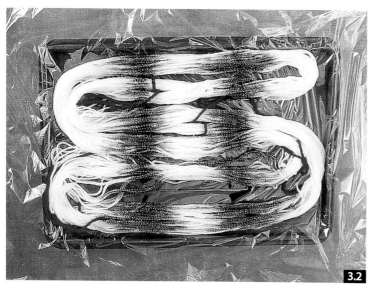

3.2

3.3

If your dishes don't have lids you can use polythene film or, for oven/hob methods, aluminium foil. For cold water dyeing, where you don't need to fit the container into the oven/microwave, a couple of plastic cat litter trays from your local pet shop are ideal. Failing that, any flat-based plastic, stainless steel, glass or enamel container will be fine, but again, avoid aluminium and iron.

3.4

Polythene film (clingfilm)

This film is required for wrapping yarns for steaming and for painting yarn. Choose a good quality, wide film. Catering film is ideal, but avoid microwaveable film as this is not usually strong enough. For this fixing method the yarn is laid out on the polythene film and the dyes applied. Once the dye has been applied, the film is wrapped around the yarn and either left to set or steamed (Fig 3.2, above).

Measuring equipment

To measure liquids for soaking solutions and dyestock solutions, you will need either a calibrated jug (Fig 3.3, top right), or a suitable set of scales .

For measuring dye powders, a set of cooks' measuring spoons is a good, cost-effective choice (Fig 3.4, above). As you will be working with small amounts of dye, choose a set which can measure as little as ¼ teaspoon (1.25ml) or as close as you can get.

Stirrers

Glass, plastic or wood sticks to stir dyebaths and poke down fibres (Fig 3.5, facing page).

3.5

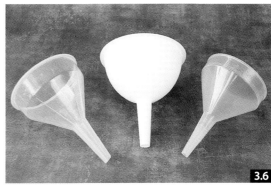

3.6

3.7

Small funnels

Not essential, but very useful for transferring dye powders and solutions to bottles with small necks (Fig 3.6, above). If you don't have a funnel for each colour, be sure to rinse and dry carefully after each colour to ensure that the dyes don't stick to the funnel and affect the next batch.

Jars/bottles

Wide-mouthed jars are good for mixing and storing made-up dye solutions (Fig 3.7, left). Remember to label, date and store away carefully in a cool, safe place out of direct sunlight. Dyes should retain full strength for at least one month, and even 12-month-old dyes will produce satisfactory colours, although they will be much paler and unrepeatable.

Labels

Instead of adhesive labels, I use translucent sticky tape (Fig 3.8, left); it looks almost white and is commonly used for photocopying, as it doesn't show through, and for book repairs as it doesn't crack or discolour with age; if you write on it with a pencil, you can erase and write new information, and it is also quite resilient to small amounts of water. Adhesive labels are, of course, a good alternative, but try to choose ones which can be removed relatively easily if you intend to re-use your dye bottles and jars.

3.8

Bottles/pipettes/basters for applying dye to the yarns

One of the easiest ways to apply dye to yarns is to make up the dye in a plastic 'sports drink' bottle with a squeezy top. The clear bottles work particularly well as you can see the dye, but be very careful about labelling, so as to avoid accidents. A permanent marker pen should write on plastic without rubbing off but, if you can't find a suitable marker to write directly onto the plastic, label as above to identify your dye containers and their contents.

Alternatively, a dedicated plastic meat baster – quite cheap from cookware/hardware shops – would hold a good amount of dye. Simply suck up the dye from a jar into the baster and squirt onto the yarn. A separate baster for each colour is best but, if your budget doesn't extend to that, rinse carefully between colours and re-use (Fig 3.9, below left).

For small amounts of colour you can use syringes or pipettes (available from pharmacists or craft shops), but this can be a bit painstaking. If all else fails simply pour the dye solution from a jug or even its own container directly onto the yarn. It lacks precision but I have used this method successfully, particularly where I have been looking for lots of colour blending with a limited amount of 'pure' colour in the final piece (Fig 3.10, below right).

Notebook

Try and keep a consistent dyeing record of all the relevant information: notes of the yarn, how much dye was used, how much water, what the application and dye method was, and so on. If possible, also keep small, labelled samples to remind yourself what the undyed and dyed yarn looked like.

There is a copy of the template I use on page 144, which you could photocopy and use to record your dye batches and methods. If you are keeping samples of your dyed yarn, cross-reference the sample to the dyeing record so you can retrieve it easily.

Access to an oven/microwave/steamer (for protein fibres)

Very few of us can afford separate heating facilities just for dyeing, so try and pick up a cheap microwave, a tabletop oven, or a portable stove ring. Otherwise, be sure to cover your yarn while it is being heated, to prevent unnecessary splashes, and clean up thoroughly after each dye session.

3.9

3.10

If you intend to steam your yarn, you will need a steamer that is dedicated to dyeing. This is because the polythene film is not sealed as such, so it is difficult to ensure that no dye can escape into the steaming water. The steamer could be the electric type, a microwave steamer or a hob-based set up.

Note

Health and Safety Guidelines

Although they are not strictly toxins or poisons, dyes – like any other chemical in your house – should be treated with great care and respect. With a few simple precautions dyes can be used quite safely, so please follow these guidelines:

1 *Avoid inhaling dye powders. Use a suitable dust mask and always handle dye powders carefully to reduce dusting.*

2 *Avoid inhaling vapours from dyepots. Work in a well-ventilated area.*

3 *Do not eat or drink while working with dyes.*

4 *Never smoke while working with dyes.*

5 *Protect your skin, clothes and your dyeing area. Staining caused by handling dye powders can be difficult to remove. Wearing gloves will also protect your hands from absorbing dye through any cuts, and so on. If you have room for a separate dyeing area (in your garage or shed, for example) that's ideal. If you must use the kitchen, cover surfaces and clean thoroughly after each dyeing session.*

6 *Keep a separate set of utensils for dyeing only. Label all your dyeing equipment (or keep clearly separated) and don't use it for cooking or other activities. The only exceptions to this are the stove and the microwave (unless you have two), which should be thoroughly cleaned after each dyeing session. Ovenproof glass dishes, jugs and jars can be bought cheaply at discount hardware shops, local charity/thrift shops or at jumble, car boot or yard sales.*

7 *Store and use dyes safely. As with all chemicals, label dyes and store well out of reach of children and animals. If dyes are accidentally ingested or splashed in the eyes, follow the manufacturer's instructions. All manufacturers will supply a dye information sheet for each of their products, so do request one when you order your dyes.*

8 *Avoid dyeing if you are, or think you may be, pregnant.*

9 *Consider the environment when disposing of dyes. In the main, the quantities of dyes you will be using will have minimum impact and small amounts of diluted dye in your rinse water should not cause any problems. However, it is advisable, particularly if you plan to dye in significant quantities, to take your unwanted dye solutions to your local disposal site where they may be dealt with according to the guidelines in your area.*

Caution

Dyeing Yarn

Rainbow dyeing

'Rainbow dyeing' is a broad term used to describe any technique in which fibres are dyed using a range of colours or shades, applied at random, to create a multi-coloured or 'rainbow' effect (see Fig 4.1, right), and this is the main technique used for the projects in this book. The beauty of this style of dyeing is that few accurate measurements are needed and yet the results, whilst they may be somewhat unpredictable, are really exciting and dramatic.

There are three key stages in the dyeing process: preparing the yarn to accept and retain the dye; applying the dye; and fixing the dye.

4.1

Preparing the yarn

Skeining

First divide the yarn into a number of skeins, depending on the number of different colours/colour combinations you want in the final design and also on the thickness of the yarn. Even if you intend to use a single colour combination, a thick yarn may need to be divided into a number of skeins to ensure that the dyes can fully penetrate the yarn. For finer yarns it is possible to work with a single skein, but first make sure that it will fit comfortably in your dyepot.

If you purchased yarn in a ball or on a cone – or if you want to divide an existing skeined yarn into smaller skeins – use either a piece of firm card, a friendly pair of hands, or a large book. Wrap the yarn (evenly, but not too tightly) around your piece of card (see Fig 4.2 left), a set number of times (I use 25 or 50, depending on the thickness of the yarn); this way, the skeins will be evenly sized and, where skeins have to be soaked/dyed in separate containers, you can work out the volume of solution required in each container by dividing the weight of the skeins into the total volume of solution.

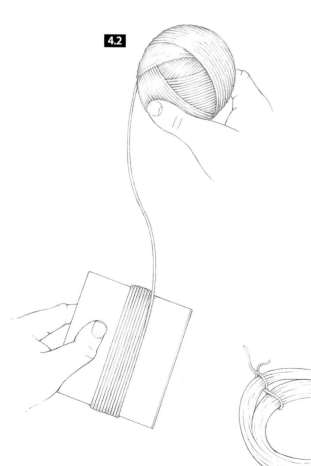

4.2

4.3

Once you have completed your wraps, tie the skein loosely in several places, in a figure of eight (Fig 4.3, left); this holds it in place but allows the dye to penetrate. Slide the yarn carefully off the card and your skein is ready for soaking.

Soaking

Before skeined yarn can be dyed, it must be soaked in water (called 'pre-soaking' or 'wetting out') to allow the yarn to absorb dye more readily. The water used to soak the yarn also carries the chemicals needed to enable the dye to penetrate the yarn more evenly and to fix the dye to the yarn, making it wash-fast.

Chemicals

For rainbow dyeing, all the necessary chemicals (other than the dyes themselves) are introduced at the pre-soaking stage. Those needed will depend on the type of dye used and the fibre being dyed. The fibre-reactive dyes used throughout this book need the following chemicals:

- for animal fibres: household salt (cooking or table) and distilled vinegar (white/pickling or preserving). Do not use malt vinegar, as it dulls the end product and makes it difficult to produce vibrant shades.

- for plant-based fibres: household salt (cooking or table) and sodium carbonate (also known as soda ash). When buying sodium carbonate, be sure to use one which is suitable for dyeing; ordinary washing soda contains brightening or whitening agents which affect the dyeing process. Soda without brighteners can be readily obtained from dye suppliers or craft shops.

What are the chemicals for?

Salt acts as a 'levelling agent', enabling the dye to penetrate the yarn more evenly, so blotchy or patchy areas are avoided in the finished yarn.

The vinegar (or soda) is the 'fixer'. As the name implies, the fixer bonds the dye to the fibre. Yarns which have not been fixed will not be reliably wash-fast and the dye may fade or even disappear completely when the finished item is washed.

Applying the dye

Dye may be applied to yarn in a wide variety of ways and the method you choose will depend on the look you want to achieve. When rainbow dyeing, the dyes are mainly applied directly to the pre-soaked fibre using bottles, pipettes or similar containers but there are, of course, a variety of other methods and some of these are mentioned on pages 48–51.

Fixing the dye

Fixers are used to make the dye bond to the fibre. For plant fibres, the soda alone will be sufficient to fix the dye to the yarn and make the dyed yarn wash-fast. This is why plant fibres can be dyed without the need for heat. Animal fibres, however, require heat as well as a fixer to ensure a good bond between the dye and the yarn. For animal fibres, therefore, the yarn is 'cooked' once the dye has been applied, using either a microwave, hob, oven or steamer to provide the necessary heat.

Rainbow dyeing using the cold and hot water methods

Before you commence dyeing, make sure that you are using the right process for the yarn you will be using: hot water for animal- (protein-) based yarns, cold water for plant- (cellulose-) based yarns. Silk, incidentally, can be dyed using either method.

Read and fully understand the Health and Safety Guidelines on page 37, and you're ready to start.

Dyeing Materials and Equipment

Fig 4.4 Materials for dyeing protein fibres

For dyeing wool and other protein fibres you will need:

The basic equipment listed on pages 33–6, plus items shown in Fig 4.4:

- Protein-based yarn (for example, wool, silk, angora, mohair, cashmere) wound into one or more skeins
- Distilled (white or pickling/preserving) vinegar
- Water
- Salt (ordinary table or cooking salt is fine)
- A selection of fibre-reactive (procion MX) dyes (between one and three colours for the projects in this book)

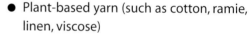

Fig 4.5 Materials for dyeing plant fibres

For dyeing cotton and other plant fibres you will need:

The basic equipment listed on pages 33–6, plus (see Fig 4.5):

- Plant-based yarn (such as cotton, ramie, linen, viscose)
- Sodium carbonate, without brighteners or whiteners (also known as soda ash)
- Water
- Salt (ordinary table or cooking salt is fine)
- A selection of fibre-reactive (procion MX) dyes (between one and three colours for the projects in this book)

Method

1 Weigh the dry yarn (Fig 4.6).

2 Using the guide in Appendix C (animal fibres) on page 146, or D (plant fibres) on page 147, calculate the quantities of water, salt and fixer required for the weight of yarn. If dark shades are required, or the yarn is very highly twisted or very thick, the quantities of salt and fixer should be doubled to ensure maximum penetration of the dye into the yarn.

If you have access to a laminator, photocopy and laminate the two calculation guides, or mount the photocopies on board and cover them with transparent adhesive film. You will then have them to hand and can wipe them clean if dye is spilt on them.

Tip

3 Put the salt and fixer in a bucket, add the water and mix thoroughly.

4 Add the yarn and soak until it is well wetted (at least 45 minutes).

5 Using the guide in Appendix E on pages 148-9, calculate the quantity of dye solution you will require, then make up your dye solution as follows:

6 Weigh the dye powder and transfer carefully to a jar, 'sports bottle' or similar container (a funnel comes in very handy here – see Fig 4.7, right). Take care not to inhale any powder and try to keep dye dust to a minimum by handling powders gently and working in a well-ventilated, but not draughty, room.

7 Gradually add the water to the dye powder and stir gently to form a paste, which will become liquid as you add more water. Keep stirring until all the powder has dissolved and all the water has been added.

Pre-soak more yarn than you need for your project, as there is often excess dye left in the dye pot and this dye (the exhaust) can be reused to dye further yarn. The resulting yarn will be a single colour – largely unpredictable and unrepeatable – which is an amalgam of all the colours used in the original dye process.

Tip

8 Label each dye, in case you forget later (see page 35). Note the dye colour and brand, strength of the solution (see Step 2, facing page), date the solution was made and the volume of solution made.

9 Repeat this process for each dye.

10 Once your yarn is wetted and your dyes are ready, you can begin the dyeing process.

11 Gently squeeze out the yarn (do not wring it), to avoid damaging delicate yarn fibres. The extent to which you squeeze out the yarn will influence the way in which the colours blend: the more wet the yarn, the greater the blending and the less distinct the individual colours are likely to be.

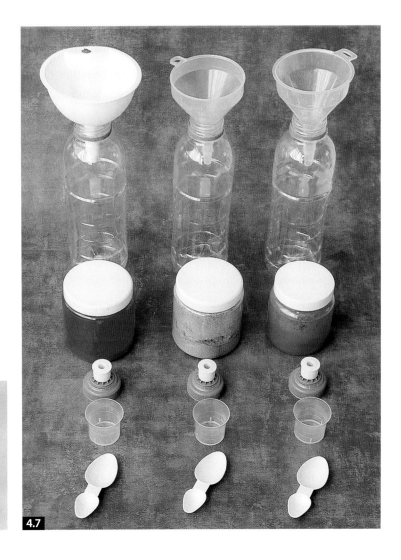

4.7

4.8

A drier yarn, on the other hand, may take more dye to achieve full coverage of the fibres, but you are more likely to be able to keep discrete areas of an individual base colour in the finished yarn.

12 Arrange the squeezed yarn in the dyepot or on a large piece of clingfilm. It can be arranged at random, coiled, or laid to and fro like a series of 's' bends (see Figs 4.8, 4.9 and 4.10, left). Yarn can be tightly packed or loose. Tightly packed yarn will require more dye and it may be necessary to use a syringe or pipette to inject it into the centre, if you want to avoid undyed patches. More loosely arranged yarn will absorb dye faster, but take care not to apply too much dye, as any excess will swill around the yarn causing the colours to muddy.

13 To apply the dyes, take one of your dye solutions and squeeze or pour the dye carefully onto the yarn. You can apply the dye in stripes (see Figs 4.11and 4.12, below and top right), in a spiral formation (Figs 4.13 and 4.14, right) or simply squirt it at random (Figs 4.15 and 4.16, bottom right).

4.9

4.10

4.11

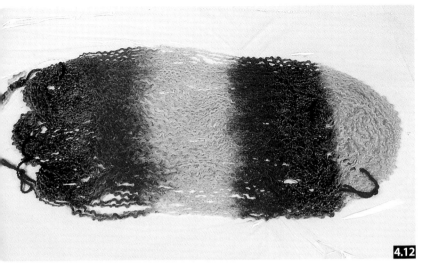

4.12

4.13

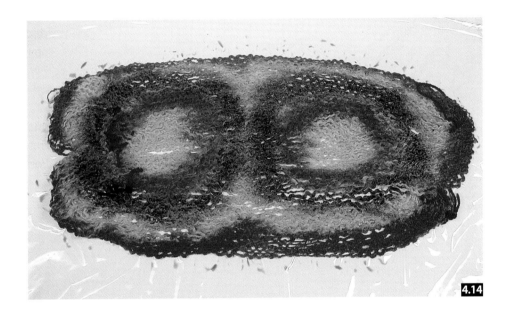

4.14

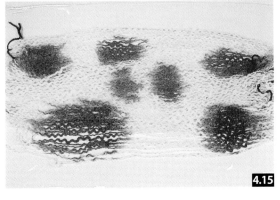

4.15

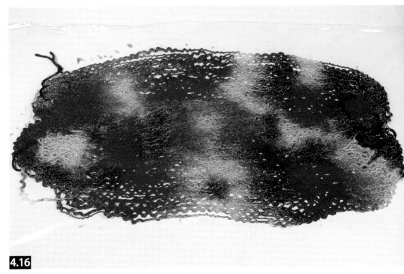

4.16

4.17

As you will see, the application of the dyes creates different effects, depending on the method used. Fig 4.17 (left) shows the skeins produced from applying the dye in stripes (top), in spirals (centre) and randomly (bottom).

As a general guide, the more random the application of the dye, the more random the effect, particularly if the yarn itself is arranged in an unstructured way. Stripes are more likely to create discrete areas of colour (Fig 4.18, below left) although any 'stripy' effect will also depend on the width of the stripes, the layout of the yarn and the distance between the stripe repeats in the finished item.

Spirals and randomly applied dyes will produce less distinct effects (Figs 4.19 and 4.20, below). If you are using a jar and baster, try sucking up some dye solution, pushing the baster into the yarn and squeezing the dye directly into the middle of the yarn (Fig 4.21, top right). A pipette or syringe can also be used in this way.

You can use up all of one colour first, apply a little of each shade in turn, or mix a little of two dyes in a separate dish then apply the mixed dye to the yarn.

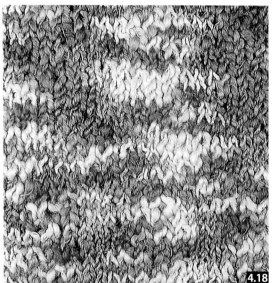

4.18

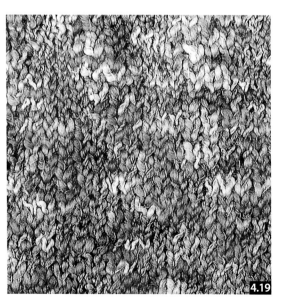

4.19

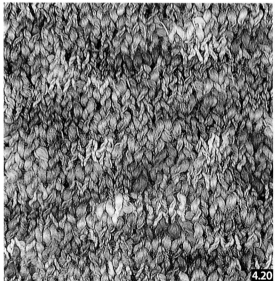

4.20

4.21

Note

If the yarn is very tightly packed or very well-squeezed, the colour may not spread as you wish, so that sections of yarn do not take up any dye. Providing you are very careful, you can encourage the dye to spread into the undyed sections by gently pressing the undyed area with a stirrer stick. However, unless you want a very blended yarn, resist the urge to poke about any more than is absolutely necessary, and under no circumstances stir the yarn about in the dye.

Alternatively, you could transfer part of one of your colours into another jar, dilute with more water and use some of this diluted shade on your yarn. The possibilities really are endless.

14 For cotton and other plant fibres, when you have finished applying your dyes, simply leave the yarn undisturbed in the dyepot or on the film for at least six hours. Then go to step 17, below.

15 For animal and other protein fibres, when you have finished applying your dyes, 'cook' your yarn as follows, bearing in mind that the time may need to be varied depending on the weight and thickness of the yarn:

In the microwave

Put the lid on the dyepot (or cover loosely with clingfilm) and cook on full power for about five to six minutes, or until the liquid is near to boiling. You may need to vary the time depending on your microwave. Check the yarn at regular intervals – it should be steaming hot, but must remain damp.

In the oven

Cover your dyepot and cook for about 20–30 minutes at 275˚F /140˚C/gas mark 1.

On the hob or stove top

Put the lid on the dyepot and heat the yarn slowly until it is almost boiling. Cover and simmer for 20–30 minutes, making sure the pot doesn't boil over or boil dry.

In the steamer

Simply fold the clingfilm carefully over the yarn and roll it up into a coil-shaped parcel (Figs 4.22 below, 4.23 and 4.24 overleaf). Place the parcels of yarn in the steamer, making sure the yarn cannot come into direct contact with the water (Fig 4.25 overleaf). Once the water has reached boiling point, steam the yarn for 20–30 minutes (or five minutes for a microwave steamer), making sure the pot doesn't boil dry.

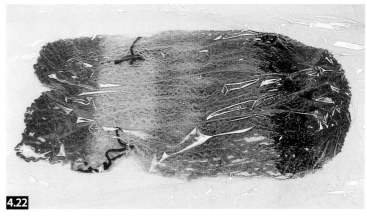
4.22

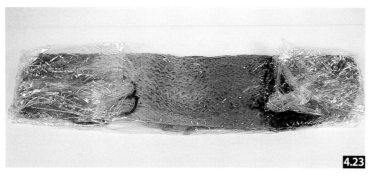

4.23

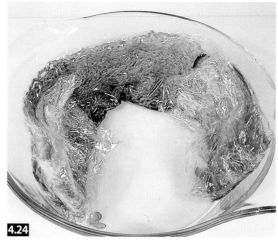

4.24

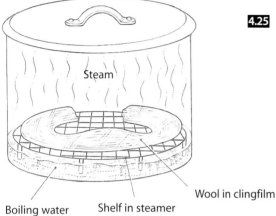

4.25

Steam

Boiling water   Shelf in steamer   Wool in clingfilm

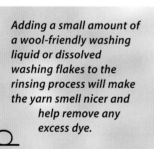

4.26

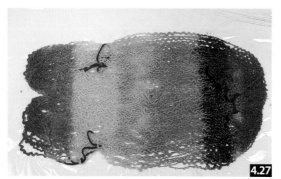

4.27

16 When your yarn is 'cooked', allow it to cool to room temperature.

17 Gently remove the yarn from the dyepot, rinse and dry (Fig 4.26, below). Remember, if you want to use the dyebath exhaust to dye more yarn, put this to one side before you start rinsing the yarn.

With time and practice you will develop your own favourite techniques. In the meantime, here is some advice based on my experience which you may find useful:

- More water equals more blending. For clearly defined colours and limited blending (such as for a 'colours of the rainbow' yarn) use well-squeezed yarn and apply dyes slowly and in small amounts to discrete areas of the yarn. Handle the yarn as little as possible. If you want more discrete colours, the steamer method tends to be easier to control, particularly if you paint the dyes onto the yarn. I find this the simplest way to produce a yarn in which you can see all the colours of the rainbow (see Fig 4.27, left). With plant fibres, too, painting the dyes on the yarn makes it easier to control the extent of any blending.

- Conversely, if you want a well-blended yarn, squeeze out less water and the dyes will blend more thoroughly. If the dyes are not blending enough, you can sprinkle on a little extra water.

- The more the muddier: too many dyes can create a muddied yarn, especially where the dyes blend. Try to limit yourself to three base colours.

- Unless you want white spots in your yarn (which in fact can look very effective), check that the dyes have fully penetrated all the yarn. This is especially important where yarns are tightly packed or tightly spun. Clear, ovenproof dishes are helpful here, as you can see whether the dye has fully penetrated the yarn by carefully lifting the dish and checking that the bottom and sides of the yarn have no white spots.

- Don't over-engineer: the more you mess with the dyepot, the more muddy the result is likely to be. Try to resist the urge to poke around too much.

- Don't despair: the least promising dyepots can produce good results, so finish off the process – including washing and drying the yarn – before you write it off as a disaster. The colour of the bath is not always indicative of the colour of the yarn, especially with a rainbow yarn where the exhaust is usually a dark brown. Once the yarn is rinsed, and the brown washed away, the jewel colours will shine through. Amazingly, the dull-looking sludge in Fig 4.28 (above) produced the lovely dyed yarns in 1.18 (see page 17) and the murky purple in 4.29 (middle) produced the lovely dark shades in Figs 1.16 and 1.17 (page 16).

Had a real disaster?

Consider overdyeing, especially if the yarn is pale. This yarn (Fig. 4.30) was too solidly pink for what I needed so I overdyed it with a small amount of cerulean blue. The resulting yarn was much more interesting and lively – some blue can be seen where the original yarn was very pale; some of the original pink remains where the colour was strong or no blue dye was applied; and there are some areas with varying degrees of purple where the blue and pink combined.

If even overdyeing doesn't do the trick, look back at your dyeing records and try to identify where things went astray, so that you can avoid repeating the mistake.

4.28

4.29

4.30

4.31

4.32

Uses for leftover dye

Don't throw surplus dye away; save it for a future project, or use it on some of the extra yarn you put in the pre-soak solution to experiment with a new technique. You could make a small amount of dye go further by diluting it and, by using progressive dilutions of a single shade, you can create some really interesting pastels. You can also use small amounts of leftover dye to colour tension squares (see Tension/Gauge, page 109) or other items.

Some alternative techniques to try

There are many different ways of applying dyes to fibres – here are just a few. Feel free to try your own, but remember to follow the Health and Safety Guidelines on page 37.

Resist or tie-dye

First, bind parts of the skein, preferably with a yarn or string made from an acrylic or other man-made fibre which won't absorb any dye. Make your ties tight, or the dye will seep through. Where the yarn is tied, it will remain in its original, undyed state. When the yarn is washed and dried, you can untie some or all

of the binders and either keep the yarn with natural areas, overdye the whole skein with a single shade of dye, or put on new ties in either the dyed or undyed sections.

Depending on how you have tied the skein at each stage, you may get areas of completely undyed yarn, areas with only the first colour, areas with only the second colour and sections which are a combination of each.

The lovely wool/silk mix yarn shown in Fig. 4.31 (above left) started life white and was dyed pink initially. For the second stage, some of the original ties were removed and some new ties added. Cerulean blue was then applied over the top.

Where the original ties remained throughout the process, the yarn has stayed white. Where ties were added at the end of the first stage, the yarn is pure pink. Where the white yarn was revealed at the end of the first stage, this yarn has taken up just the cerulean blue. Areas where the cerise pink was left exposed after stage one are purple, being a combination of the pink from stage one and cerulean blue from stage two.

Dip-dyeing

As the name implies, for this method the yarn is simply dipped into the dye, either using a single dyepot, or by lining up several pots of different colours (see Fig 4.32 above and Fig 4.33 on facing page). It can be quite a messy process, so cover up with extra care.

4.33

4.34

Dip-dyeing can be particularly effective with chenille yarns, as shown in Fig 4.34 (right). This yarn was originally the very pale green-blue, which I obtained using the exhaust from another dye batch. I wasn't happy with it, so I made up a small amount of purple dye and dipped the ends of the skein into it. The yarn soaked up the purple very quickly and I had to hold it up to stop the purple completely covering it. You can see in the picture where the yarn was in direct contact with the purple, darkening it, and where the dye has spread into the blue, giving a more delicate violet/blue-green shade.

If you want the dye to wick up into the yarn using this method, it needs to be quite wet. Viscose and most protein yarns lend themselves well to the dip-dyeing technique. However, cotton and other plant fibres are less susceptible to this wick effect and the degree of spread of the dye may be much less, even if the yarn is quite wet.

Yarn painting

For this method, the yarn should be laid on a large piece of clingfilm, as for the steaming method. Using a large, soft paintbrush, carefully paint dye onto one side of the yarn (Fig 4.35, right). Turn the yarn over gently and paint the other side. Check that the dye has penetrated all the yarn, then fold the clingfilm over the yarn and either steam or simply leave to set, depending on the yarn

being used. If you are using different colour dyes, it is best to use a different brush for each colour but, if this is not possible, make sure you rinse your brush thoroughly between each colour.

Spray painting

Very interesting effects can be achieved using this method, but it is a messy process. You will need a large box in which to spray the yarn – to prevent any stray dye being sprayed everywhere – and a sprayer, such as a clean plant spray or a compressed air unit.

First, rig up a system to hold the yarn: two sticks poked through the back of the box to

4.35

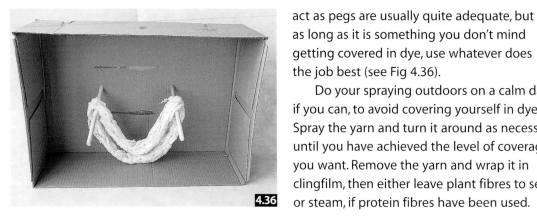

4.36

act as pegs are usually quite adequate, but as long as it is something you don't mind getting covered in dye, use whatever does the job best (see Fig 4.36).

Do your spraying outdoors on a calm day, if you can, to avoid covering yourself in dye. Spray the yarn and turn it around as necessary, until you have achieved the level of coverage you want. Remove the yarn and wrap it in clingfilm, then either leave plant fibres to set, or steam, if protein fibres have been used.

Overdyeing

I mentioned overdyeing as a possible solution for dealing with an unwanted colour or dyeing disaster (see page 47). It can also be used to create interesting effects in its own right.

4.37

4.38

4.39

4.40

You can overdye an existing dyed yarn, or a naturally coloured yarn (there are many beautiful greys and browns in the natural yarn spectrum which can be very satisfactorily overdyed). The skeins in Fig. 4.37, on the facing page, were originally a white Shetland yarn, whereas the yarns in Figs 4.38 and 4.39 were grey and brown respectively. Certain silks also come in shades other than white and produce equally stunning effects (Fig. 4.40).

Bear in mind the effect that the original colour will have on your final shade, as you may need to compensate for this. Primaries red, yellow and blue used on a grey or brown Shetland wool, for example, produce much softer shades than the same dyes used on a pure white Shetland yarn (Fig. 4.42, below right).

Silks are also very different when a coloured silk is used rather than a bleached silk. Compare the dyed and undyed natural coloured silks on the left in Fig 4.41 (below left) with the dyed and undyed bleached silks on the right in the same picture: notice that the colours of the natural coloured silk are much more subtle than the vibrant shades of the bleached silk.

Combining techniques

The various dyeing methods are not mutually exclusive and it can be fun combining them: try wrapping part of a skein before spray dyeing, then unwrap, wrap another area and spray with a different colour; or dip-dye your skeins with a very pale colour, then overspray with a different shade in the same colour family.

4.41

4.42

If you are using a very expensive yarn, test a small skein before proceeding with the full process. You can then experiment freely whilst limiting the cost of any results you don't like.

Note

Before you start

These projects are based around simple shapes which have been created using the minimum of stitches and techniques. If you are unfamiliar with the stitches specified, or any of the processes, Back to Basics (see pages 107–31) has full instructions on everything you should need, from casting on, to making up.

The knitting and crochet projects are separated out, and arranged progressively:

indicates that the project could easily be attempted by a complete novice

indicates that the project is straightforward, but may involve some basic shaping techniques

indicates that the project is more challenging, and requires a little patience and attention to the pattern.

Details of the dye recipes, colours used and techniques are included for each project and, if you follow the instructions exactly, the overall colour scheme and proportions should be broadly similar to those used in my samples, but still unique: the beauty of this process is that it is virtually impossible to produce two identical rainbow-dyed pieces.

Experimentation is a hugely enjoyable part of the whole process so, if you wish to substitute yarn, see page 12; if you wish to substitute colours, see the guide to colour theory (page 25) and the standard dyeing instructions (page 38), then use the patterns as a template for your own custom-made creations.

Above all, have fun!

The Projects

Knitting Projects

PROJECT 1

Colourful
Woolly Scarf

Scarf size

Approx. 8in wide x 51in long (20 x 130cm)

Materials and equipment for dyeing

Basic equipment listed on pages 33–6, plus:

6oz (180g) 4ply wool yarn divided into
    4 skeins of 1¹/₂oz (45g) each

1¹/₂oz (45g) salt

³/₄ cup (180ml) white vinegar

1¹/₂ gal (5.4l) water

¹/₂tsp (2.5ml) procion mx dye brilliant
    pink mx-5b made up into a 1%
    solution (¹/₂tsp [2.5ml] dye and 1 cup
    [250ml] water)

¹/₂tsp (2.5ml) procion mx dye royal blue
    mx-r made up into a 1% solution
    (¹/₂tsp [2.5ml] dye and 1 cup [250ml]
    water)

¹/₂tsp (2.5ml) procion mx dye cerulean
    blue mx-g made up into a 1% solution
    (¹/₂tsp [2.5ml] dye and 1 cup [250ml]
    water)

*This scarf is knitted in moss stitch and,
as you can see, it looks surprisingly fancy
and stylish, even though it is a simple pattern
which uses just knit and purl stitches. There
is no shaping or making up and, even if you
are a knitting novice, you can knit this in
a couple of evenings.*

*You can of course, change the length just
by working more or fewer rows and choose
colour combinations suitable for all ages
and tastes. For those who like something with
a little added panache, try customizing the
scarf with some tassels on the corners,
or perhaps work in some contrasting
metallic yarn at the beginning and
end, and incorporate some
metallic yarn or beads
into the tassels (see
pages 132–5).*

55

Colourful Woolly Scarf

Dyeing the yarn

Method

1 In a large bucket, dissolve the salt and vinegar in the water. Soak all four skeins for at least 45 minutes in this solution.

2 While the yarn is soaking, make up each of the three dyes into a 1% strength stock solution using ½tsp (2.5ml) dye and 1 cup (250ml) water for each colour, following the instructions in Appendix E (see page 148).

3 Skein 1: squeeze out the prepared wet yarn and coil it in a dish, but leave enough liquid in the dish to reach just below the top of the yarn. Apply the dye randomly, using roughly equal amounts of the two blue shades, but more of the pink colour; this should produce a muted, well-blended shade with few discrete areas of the individual dyes, as the water will dilute the dyes and allow them to mix freely. The use of more pink in the mix should produce a range of predominantly pink shades.

4 Skeins 2 and 3: squeeze the prepared yarn until it has stopped dripping, then coil it in a dish. Randomly apply an equal amount of each dye to the yarn. This will produce a bright yarn, with both areas where the dyes have mixed and areas of of pure colour from a single dye. (The use of less water allows the dyes to mix to some extent, forming purples and similar shades, but does not dilute the colours, so that a more vibrant, dramatic look is achieved.)

5 Skein 4: gently squeeze out the prepared, wet yarn until well wetted but not dripping, then coil it in a dish and apply dye randomly, using more of the blues than the pink, then sprinkle further water onto parts of the skein. Where there is more water, greater colour-blending occurs, resulting in a more muted shade; the blues create a predominantly purple shade-range (in contrast to skein 1), but some areas of pure colour are retained where there was no additional water.

It is not necessary to use all of each of the solutions so, once the dyes have been applied and you are happy with the result, move on to the 'cooking' process to set the yarn. Depending on the 'cooking' method you are using, cover the yarn (or wrap in clingfilm and place in the steamer) then either:

> Microwave for 5–6 minutes
> Cook in the oven on low heat for 20 minutes
> Cook on the hob for 20 minutes
> Steam for 20 minutes (5 minutes if steaming in microwave)

Allow the cooked yarn to cool, then remove carefully from the container/s, rinse thoroughly and allow to dry.

To knit the scarf

Equipment

One pair size 5 needles (3¾mm, old UK size 9) or size required to achieve the stated tension.

Tension

22 sts and 39 rows worked in moss st (see below) should produce a 4in (10cm) square (but see Tension/Gauge, on page 109).

Using size 5 needles (3¾mm, old UK size 9) cast on 45 sts. Work 264 rows (approx. 51in [130cm]), changing between your skeins at irregular intervals to form uneven stripes and working each row as follows:

*K1, P1, rep from * to last st, K1 (i.e. always ending with K st as last st on each row). Cast off.

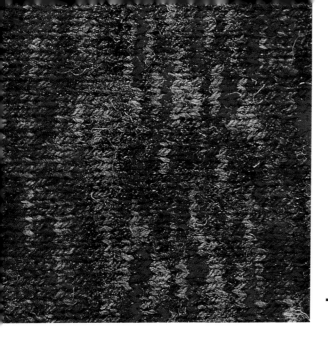

Tasselled Wool Hat

This charming hat is made of just two rectangles, knitted in stocking stitch, and is very easy to make. There is no shaping, the tassels are optional and, by varying the size, colours and embellishments, a version can be made to suit anyone in the family. A child's version, using bells or beads instead of tassels, would make an attractive option, but make sure the embellishments are firmly fastened on, as small inquisitive fingers may find them irresistible. It teams up very well with the previous scarf project.

Hat size

To fit an average lady's head
Circumference of the head – measured around the widest part – 21½in (55cm), by 14½in (37cm) long (but see 'Adjusting the size', on page 61)

Materials and equipment for dyeing

Basic equipment listed on pages 33–6, plus:

3oz (90g) 4ply wool yarn divided into 4 skeins of ¾oz approx. (20g) each

¾oz (22.5g) salt

⅓ cup (90ml) white vinegar

¾gal (2.7l) water

½tsp (2.5ml) procion mx dye brilliant pink mx-5b made up into a 1% solution (½tsp [2.5ml] dye and 1 cup [250ml] water)

½tsp (2.5ml) procion mx dye royal blue mx-r made up into a 1% solution (½tsp [2.5ml] dye and 1 cup [250ml] water)

½tsp (2.5ml) procion mx dye cerulean blue mx-g made up into a 1% solution (½tsp [2.5ml] dye and 1 cup [250ml] water)

Dyeing the yarn

Method

1 In a large bucket, dissolve the salt and vinegar in the water and soak all four skeins for at least 45 minutes in this solution.

2 While the yarn is soaking make up each of the three dyes into a 1% strength solution using ½tsp (2.5ml) dye and 1 cup (250ml) water for each colour following the instructions in Appendix E (see page 148).

3 Skein 1: squeeze out the prepared, wet yarn and coil in a dish, leaving enough liquid in the dish to reach just below the top of the yarn. Apply the dye randomly using broadly equal amounts of the two blue shades, but more of the pink colour. This should produce a muted, well-blended shade with few discrete areas of the individual dyes, as the water will dilute the dyes and allow them to mix freely. The use of more pink in the mix should produce a range of predominantly pink shades.

4 Skeins 2 and 3: squeeze the prepared yarn until it has stopped dripping, then coil it in a dish. Randomly apply an equal amount of each dye to the yarn. This will produce a bright yarn with both areas where the dyes have mixed and areas of pure colour from a single dye. (The use of less water allows the dyes to mix to some extent, forming purples and similar shades, but does not dilute the colours, so a more vibrant, dramatic look is achieved.)

5 Skein 4: squeeze out the prepared, wet yarn until well wetted but not dripping, then coil it in a dish and apply dye randomly using more of the blues than the pink, then sprinkle further water onto parts of the skein; where there is more water, greater colour blending occurs, resulting in a more muted shade: the blues create a predominantly purple shade-range (in contrast to skein 1), but some areas of pure colour are retained where there was no additional water.

It is not necessary to use all of each of the solutions so, once the dyes have been applied and you are happy with the result, move on to the 'cooking' process to set the yarn. Depending on the 'cooking' method you are using, cover the yarn (or wrap in clingfilm and place in the steamer) then either:

> Microwave for 5–6 minutes
> Cook in the oven on low heat for 20 minutes
> Cook on the hob for 20 minutes
> Steam for 20 minutes (5 minutes if steaming in microwave)

Allow the cooked yarn to cool, then remove carefully from the container/s, rinse thoroughly and allow to dry.

To knit the hat

Equipment

One pair size 5 needles (3¾mm, old UK size 9) or size required to achieve the stated tension.

Note

Alternative yarns
This pattern can be adapted to suit a variety of yarns. If your yarn tension doesn't match that of the pattern exactly, work out how many stitches you will need by making a tension square – using your preferred yarn and an appropriate size of needles – according to the instructions in **Back to Basics, page 109,** *and* **Appendix H, on page 152.**
Count the number of stitches in 4in (10cm); multiply this figure by the circumference of the head to find the total number of stitches needed, then divide the figure by two to find the number of stitches you need for each of the two pieces. For a snugger-fitting hat, deduct ½–1in (1–2cm) from the head circumference before doing your calculations.

Tension

23 sts and 29 rows worked in st st should produce a 4in (10cm) square (but see Tension/Gauge, on page 109).

Work in unequal stripes, alternating between the skeins. For the length, simply work until the hat measures 14½in (37cm) long, ignoring the number of rows and adjusting the positioning of the stripes as required.

Adjusting the size

As a guide, the length should be roughly two thirds of the circumference measurement. If the hat is for a man, it will look more in proportion if you add an inch or so (a couple of centimetres) to the length. If the hat is for a baby or small child, shorten the length to suit in the same way.

Pattern note

Stocking stitch (st st) worked thus:
Knit 1 row, purl 1 row.
Repeat these 2 rows throughout.
Both sides of the hat follow the same pattern, so make two pieces thus:
Using size 5 needles (3¾mm, old UK size 9) cast on 58 sts. Work 110 rows (approx. 14½in [37cm]) st st as follows:-

Sk 2	20 rows
Sk 4	8 rows
Sk 3	6 rows
Sk 1	8 rows
Sk 4	4 rows
Sk 3	14 rows
Sk 1	4 rows
Sk 2	6 rows
Sk 4	10 rows
Sk 1	8 rows
Sk 3	6 rows
Sk 1	12 rows
Sk 3	2 rows
Sk 2	2 rows

Cast off.

Making up

With RS tog backstitch across cast off edges of hat. With RS tog stitch side seams working from cast off edge towards cast on edge, stitching to within 2in (5cm) of cast on edge. Turn work inside out and stitch the last 2in (5cm) with WS tog (this is to make the rolled brim neater). Make two tassels (see page 132 for instructions) and attach one to each of the top corners of the hat.

Rustic Floor Cushion

Cushions are a good way to ring the changes with colour, or to jazz up a relatively subtle colour scheme. They are also useful as extra sitting space, if filled with quite a firm stuffing. Ready-made cushion pads are the quickest and simplest way but, if you prefer, you could make your own.

The front of this cushion is knitted in stocking stitch in three simple strips. The back is knitted in two pieces, designed to overlap to allow a cushion pad to be inserted. The ribbed section at the end of each piece on the back is designed to give enough stretch to insert the pad, springing back into place afterwards to keep the back closed.

I used dyed strips and plain yarn to illustrate how the two can be effectively combined, but you could use two contrasting dyed yarns, combine a commercially dyed yarn with your own dyed yarn, or make the whole cushion using different combinations of your chosen dyes.

To produce the muted shades, I prepared the dyes using a two-stage process, first making standard 1% stock solutions, and then mixing these in varying proportions, adding more water where required to produce more subtle, autumn shades. This is why the equipment list includes extra jars and basters. You can manage without the basters if you're not worried about being too precise, but make sure that the jars can hold the required volume of solution.

Cushion size
Approx. 20 x 20in (50 x 50cm)

Materials and equipment for dyeing
Basic equipment listed on pages 33–6, plus:

36oz (1,080g) pure wool super chunky yarn (set aside 24oz [720g] which will be left undyed and make two skeins of 6oz [180g] each with the remaining yarn)

3oz (90g) salt

1½cups (360ml) white vinegar

2¾gal (10.8l) water

½tsp (2.5ml) procion mx dye black mx-k, made up into a 1% solution (½tsp [2.5ml] dye and 1 cup [250ml] water)

½tsp (2.5ml) procion mx dye brilliant emerald mx-g made up into a 1% solution (½tsp [2.5ml] dye and 1 cup [250ml] water)

½tsp (2.5ml) procion mx dye lemon yellow mx-4g made up into a 1% solution (½tsp [2.5ml] dye and 1 cup [250ml] water)

½tsp (2.5ml) procion mx dye orange-scarlet mx-g made up into a 1% solution (½tsp [2.5ml] dye and 1 cup [250ml] water)

5 jars to contain mixed dyes (each with 1 cup [250ml] capacity)

Basters/pipettes/syringes to apply dye from jars to yarn (optional)

Dyeing the yarn

Method

1 Set aside 24oz (720g) of the undyed yarn (yarn B). This will remain undyed. Divide the remaining 12oz (360g) of yarn into two skeins of approximately 6oz (180g) each (yarn A).

2 In a large bucket, dissolve the salt and vinegar in the water. Soak the two skeins to be dyed for at least 45 minutes in this solution.

3 While the yarn is soaking, make up each of the dyes into a 1% strength stock solution following the instructions in Appendix E (see page 148).

4 Once the stock solutions have been prepared, mix the following combinations into the spare jars:

- $2\frac{1}{2}$ fl oz (80ml) scarlet + 6tsp (30ml) black + 2tsp (10ml) emerald, topped up with water to 1 cup (250ml)

- 8tsp (40ml) yellow + $2\frac{1}{2}$ fl oz (80ml) scarlet + 2tsp (10ml) emerald, topped up with water to $\frac{1}{2}$ cup (125ml)

- 10tsp (50ml) yellow + 1tsp (5ml) black, topped up with water to $\frac{2}{3}$ cup (160ml)

- $2\frac{1}{2}$ fl oz (80ml) scarlet + 10tsp (50ml) yellow, topped up with water to $\frac{1}{2}$ cup (125ml)

- 6tsp (30ml) emerald + 2tsp (10ml) scarlet, topped up with water to 1 cup (250ml)

5 Skeins 1 and 2: lightly squeeze the wet yarn and pile it in a dish. Apply the dye randomly, using broadly equal amounts of each of the colours, to produce a muted, well-blended shade of autumn/terracotta red with few discrete areas of the individual dyes.

6 As the yarn is thick, turn it over in the dish two or three times during the course of applying the dyes, to ensure full penetration. Have a quick check in areas where the yarn is most piled up just to ensure that the dye has penetrated to the middle of the yarn.

It is not necessary to use up all of the dye so, once the dyes have been applied and you are happy with the result, move on to the 'cooking' process to set the yarn. Depending on the 'cooking' method you are using, cover the yarn (or wrap in clingfilm and place in the steamer) then either:

Microwave for 5–6 minutes
Cook in the oven on low heat for 30 minutes
Cook on the hob for 30 minutes
Steam for 30 minutes (5 minutes if using a microwave steamer)

Allow the yarn to cool then remove carefully from the container/s, rinse thoroughly and allow to dry.

To knit the cushion

Equipment

One pair each of size 9 (5.5mm, old UK size 5) and 10 (6mm, old UK size 4) needles or sizes required to achieve the stated tension.

Tension

13 sts and 16 rows, worked in st st on size 10 needles, should produce a 4in (10cm) square (but see Tension/Gauge, on page 109).

Front
Worked in three strips
Strip 1
Using size 10 needles (6mm, old UK size 4) cast on 22 sts. Work 80 rows (20in/51cm) changing between your skeins at irregular intervals and working in st st (one row knit, one row purl). Cast off.

Strips 2 and 3

Using size 10 needles (6mm, old UK size 4) cast on 22 sts.

Using yarn A (coloured yarn), work 8 rows st st. Change to yarn B (undyed yarn), work 8 rows st st.

Repeat this pattern, changing yarns every 8 rows until 80 rows (20in/51cm) have been completed. You should have 10 blocks of alternating coloured and plain yarn.

Back

Work two pieces alike.

Using size 10 needles (6mm, old UK size 4) cast on 66 sts and work 46 rows st st. Change to size 9 (the smaller size needles) and work 8 rows K1, P1 rib. Cast off.

Making up

With RS together, backstitch the long edge of one of the striped strips to the long edge of the single colour strip. Matching the stripes across the front, with RS together, backstitch the long edge of the second striped strip to the other long side of the single colour strip (Fig 5.1).

So that the decorative stitching shows on the right side of the cushion, place the front and backs with WS together, and with the rib edges overlapping in the middle at right angles to the strips on the front (Fig 5.2). Using the undyed yarn, firmly overcast the back to the front across the top and bottom of the cushion (parallel with the ribbing).

Now turn the pieces RS tog. Pin the back pieces to the front. The ribbed sections of the two back pieces should overlap by about 22 rows (Fig 5.3).

Firmly backstitch the side seams, stitching through all three layers where the two back pieces overlap and are joined to the front. Be particularly careful to make the stitches at the edge of the overlap close together and firm.

5.1

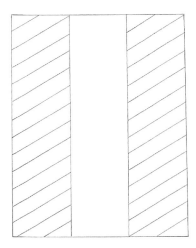

top

5.2

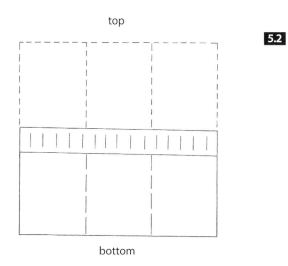

bottom

top

5.3

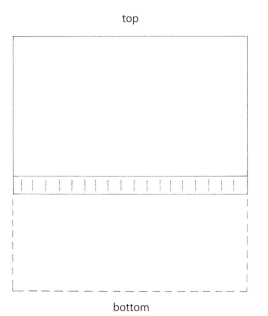

bottom

You may find it necessary to work a couple of stitches over one another at the very edge of the overlap, as this will be the greatest area of strain on the fabric when the cushion pad is inserted/removed. To start and finish off, turn the work inside out and work the start and finishing on the WS of the cushion in the normal way. Turn right way out and insert cushion pad.

The front

The back

Tip

If your ribbed edge is too loose, or if it stretches over time, use three or four large nylon/plastic snap fasteners, or some hook and loop strips to hold the back edges more neatly in place.

Note

The overcasting is intended to be a decorative stitch, which is why the stitching of the back to the front is carried out on the right side of the work. However, it is necessary to start and finish stitching on the wrong side in the normal way to avoid any unsightly yarn ends/darns.

Afghan Blanket in Patchwork Squares

Blanket size

Approx. 26½in wide x 38in long
(67 x 96.5cm)

Materials and equipment for dyeing

Basic equipment listed on pages 33–6, plus:

25oz (750g) Aran wool yarn divided into
10 skeins of approx. 2½oz (75g) each

6¼oz (187.5g) salt

3⅛ cups (750ml) white vinegar

5¾gal (22.5l) water

1tsp (5ml) procion mx dye deep purple
mx-1

1tsp (5ml) procion mx dye brilliant pink
mx-5b

¼tsp (1.25ml) procion mx dye black
mx-k

9 jars/bottles, each capable of holding
1 cup (250ml) dye solution

*Afghans are so simple that they are truly
a pleasure to make. Patchwork afghans
have the added advantage of being made
up of small, very portable pieces, which can
easily be made on the move. They are also
a great way of using up oddments of wool.*

*The size of a patchwork afghan is
almost infinitely variable. These instructions
produce a size suitable for a small settee
'throw', a baby's pram blanket, or perhaps as
a lap-blanket for taking off the chill on cool
evenings. To vary the size, simply make more
or fewer squares, but remember to adjust
the amount of yarn and dye needed.*

*Don't be put off by the apparently long
list of dyes; in fact there are just two main
dyes (brilliant pink and deep purple), with
a small amount of black. The colour changes
are achieved simply by using varying dilutions
of the pink and the purple and adding a
little bit of black to tone down colours for
some of the shades.*

Dyeing the yarn

Method

1. In a large bucket (or several smaller buckets), dissolve the salt and vinegar in the water. (If using several buckets, be sure to divide the salt, water and vinegar equally between the buckets.) Soak all skeins for at least 45 minutes in this solution.

2. While the yarn is soaking, make up each of the dyes into the appropriate strength solution as stated below, following the instructions in Appendix E (see page 148):

   a. 1 cup (250ml) procion mx dye deep purple at 1% solution (1/2tsp [2.5ml] dye and 1 cup [250ml] water)

   b. 1 cup (250ml) procion mx dye deep purple at 0.5% solution (1/4tsp [1.25ml] dye and 1 cup [250ml] water)

   c. 1 cup (250ml) procion mx dye deep purple at 0.25% solution (1/8tsp [0.625ml] dye and 1 cup [250ml] water)

   d. 1 cup (250ml) procion mx dye deep purple at 0.125% solution (1/16tsp dye [0.31ml] and 1 cup [250ml] water)

   e. 1 cup (250ml) procion mx dye brilliant pink at 1% solution (1/2tsp [2.5ml] dye and 1 cup [250ml] water)

   f. 1 cup (250ml) procion mx dye brilliant pink at 0.5% solution (1/4tsp [1.25ml] dye and 1 cup [250ml] water)

   g. 1 cup (250ml) procion mx dye brilliant pink at 0.25% solution (1/8tsp [0.625ml] dye and 1 cup [250ml] water)

   h. 1 cup [250ml] procion mx dye brilliant pink at 0.125% solution (1/16tsp [0.31ml] dye and 1 cup [250ml] water)

   i. 1/2 cup (125ml) procion mx dye black made up into a 1% solution (1/4tsp [1.25ml] dye and 1/2 cup [125ml] water)

You should now have nine bottles/jars of dye, four purple and four brilliant pink at varying dilutions, and one black at the standard 1% dilution.

Note

For dilutions where very small amounts of dye powder are required, estimate 1/4tsp as half of a 2.5ml spoon to give 1.25ml, and 1/8tsp as one quarter of a 2.5ml spoon to give 0.625ml dye powder. For these purposes, dye amounts are not absolutely critical and need not be completely accurate, so do not worry if you do not have scales capable of weighing such small amounts.

3. Skeins 1–2: squeeze the yarn gently, leaving it quite wet. Lay in a horseshoe-shape and apply dyes d, h and i along the line of the yarn. Gently squeeze the yarn, lifting it as necessary to check that the dye has penetrated through to all the fibres, adding more dye if required, to produce a muted shade, enhanced by the sparing use of black.

4. Skeins 3–4: squeeze the yarn gently, leaving it quite wet. Lay in a horseshoe-shape and apply dyes i, a and d, working across the yarn in stripes. Gently lift and squeeze the yarn as necessary to ensure that the dye has penetrated through to all the fibres; add more dye if required, to produce purples ranging from deep to pale, each softened by both the sparing use of black and by the wet yarn.

5. Skein 5: squeeze the yarn gently, leaving it quite wet. Lay in a horseshoe-shape and apply dyes e, g, a and c, working across the yarn in stripes. Gently lift and squeeze the yarn as necessary to ensure that the

dye has penetrated through to all the fibres, adding more dye if required. The use of strong purple and pink should produce vibrant colours, toned down slightly by the additional use of the diluted versions of each colour and the wet yarn.

6   Skein 6: squeeze the yarn more thoroughly until it is no longer dripping. Lay the yarns in a 'snaking formation' in the dish. Apply dyes e, g and i randomly across the yarn. Gently lift and squeeze the yarn as necessary to ensure that the dye has penetrated through to all the fibres, adding more dye if required.

7   Skein 7: squeeze the yarn until it is no longer dripping. Lay the yarns in a 'snaking formation' in the dish. Using dyes b and f, work across the yarn, covering a third of the yarn in dye b, but leaving the centre third undyed for the moment, then dye the final third with dye f. Using dyes b and f, 'fill in' the undyed centre third to create a central area which is broadly an equal mix of the two dyes. Where the centre section meets the other sections you should get a graduated transition from b through b/f to f.

Gently lift and squeeze the yarn as necessary, to ensure that the dye has penetrated through to all the fibres but, in order to maintain the transition effect,

check one colour first, adding the appropriate dye very carefully if needed. Then, wash any dye off your gloves and repeat the process for the other colour. In the centre, use a mix of the two dyes to preserve the balance of colours; do not stray too far into the transition area or the pure colours, or you will lose the transition effect.

8   Skein 8: these skeins use the same method as for skein 7 above, but use dyes a and c.

9   Skein 9: squeeze the yarn until it is no longer dripping. Lay in a horseshoe-shape and apply dyes a, c and f, working across the yarn in stripes and using the pink dye (f) only sparingly as a highlight. The yarn should be predominantly purple with occasional pink highlights.

10 Skein 10: squeeze the yarn until it is no longer dripping. Lay in a horseshoe-shape and apply dyes b, f and h, working across the yarn in quite distinct stripes, but using f fairly sparingly. This skein has clear sections of purple and pink with the intensity of shades varying from quite deep pink to a pale lilac.

It is not necessary to use all of each of the solutions so, once the dyes have been applied and you are happy with the result, move on to the 'cooking' process to set the yarn. Depending on the 'cooking' method you are using, cover the yarn (or wrap in clingfilm and place in the steamer) then either:

Microwave for 5–6 minutes
Cook in the oven for 20 minutes
Cook on the hob for 15 minutes
Steam for 20 minutes (5 minutes if steaming in microwave)

Allow the cooked yarn to cool then remove carefully from the container/s, rinse thoroughly and allow to dry.

To knit the blanket

Equipment

One pair size 10.5 needles (6.5mm, old UK size 3) or size required to achieve the stated tension.

Tension

22 sts and 17 rows worked in K2, P2 rib (see below) should produce a 4in (10cm) square (but see Tension/Gauge, on page 109).

Make 24 squares in all. Work each square as follows, working from either a single skein, or using two or more skeins together if preferred in 'imaginary' stripes:

Using size 10.5 needles (6.5mm, old UK size 3) cast on 34 sts. Work in K2, P2 rib thus:

Row 1: *K2, P2 repeat from * to last 2 sts, K2.
Row 2: *P2, K2 repeat from * to last 2 sts, P2.
Repeat these 2 rows until 25 rows have been worked in total. Cast off (not too tightly).

Making up

Lay the squares out on a large work surface and rearrange them until you are happy with the colours and the way they relate to each other. Pin a number on each square, working consistently from top left to top right (second row left to second row right, and so on) until you reach the bottom right corner. Take squares one and two and place them RS together with the ribs at right angles to one another, as shown in Fig 6.1. Overcast along one side.

Take square three and place it so that the rib is at right angles to square two. With RS together overcast square two to square three along one side. Continue in the same way, until the first row of four squares has been completed. Work the remaining rows in the same way, ensuring that the ribbing is at right angles both to the square above in row one and to the adjacent square.

When all the rows have been completed, with RS together, join all six rows to form a blanket four squares wide by six squares long.

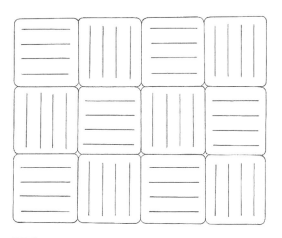

6.1

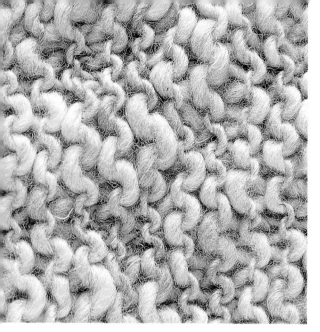

Super-chunky Child's Jumper

This attractive unisex jumper would make a good transition from the scarf (Project 1) and blanket squares (Project 4) to a first garment, particularly as it is worked entirely in garter stitch.

It has many advantages: it is extremely quick to make; there is very little shaping, yet the style doesn't look 'blocky'; the slubby wool yarn gives warmth without excess weight; and its springy texture will withstand being crumpled up in a rucksack or stuffed in a holdall, yet still look presentable.

Jumper size

To fit a child age 6–7 (chest 32in/80cm)

Materials and equipment for dyeing

Basic equipment listed on pages 33–6, plus:

20oz (600g) slubby pure wool DK yarn divided into 6 skeins of approximately 3¹⁄₂oz (100g) each

5oz (150g) salt

2¹⁄₂ cups (600ml) white vinegar

4¹⁄₂gal (18l) water

1tsp (5ml) procion mx dye lemon yellow mx-g

1tsp (5ml) procion mx dye bright emerald green mx-g

¹⁄₂tsp (2.5ml) procion mx dye black mx-k

9 jars/bottles, each capable of holding 2 cups (500ml) dye solution

Dyeing the yarn

Method

1 Divide the yarn into 6 skeins of approximately 3½oz (100g) each.

2 In a large bucket, dissolve the salt and vinegar in the water. (If using several smaller buckets, divide the salt, water and vinegar equally between them.) Soak all skeins for at least 45 minutes in this solution.

3 While the yarn is soaking make up each of the dyes into the appropriate strength solution as stated below, following the instructions in Appendix E (see page 148):

Make up 1 cup (250ml) of each of the dyes (yellow, green and black) into 1% solutions in separate bottles (½tsp [2.5ml] dye and 1 cup [250ml] water in each one).

These dye solutions are then used to make the following six combinations:

1 ⅓ cup (90ml) lemon yellow
   2tsp (10ml) black
   top up with water to make 1¼ cup (300ml) dye solution

2 3½ fl oz (100ml) bright emerald green
   3½ fl oz (100ml) black
   top up with water to make 1¼ cup (300ml) dye solution

3 3½ fl oz (100ml) bright emerald green
   2tsp (10ml) black
   top up with water to make 2 cups (500ml) dye solution

4 5tsp (25ml) bright emerald green top up with water to make 10tsp (50ml) dye solution

5 3½ fl oz (100ml) black

6 5 fl oz (150ml) lemon yellow

Lay each skein in a horseshoe-shape in a dish and apply the six dye solutions as follows:

Skeins 1–6: leaving the skeins damp but not dripping, apply some of each of the six dyes to each of the skeins at random, varying the proportions of each colour used as desired. As the yarn is thick and bulky, turn the yarn to ensure that the dye has fully penetrated to the centre of the skein.

To achieve a well-blended range of shades, the yarn can be squeezed gently to encourage the dyes to blend into one another. For more distinct separation of shades, use less squeezing.

It is not necessary to use all of each of the solutions so, once the dyes have been applied and you are happy with the result, move onto the 'cooking' process to set the yarn. Depending on the 'cooking' method you are using, cover the yarn (or wrap in clingfilm and place in the steamer) then either:

Microwave for 5–6 minutes
Cook in the oven for 20 minutes
Cook on the hob for 15 minutes
Steam for 20 minutes (5 minutes if using a microwave steamer)

Allow the cooked yarn to cool, then remove carefully from the container/s, rinse thoroughly and allow to dry.

To knit the jumper

Equipment

One pair size 13 needles (9mm, old UK size 00) or size required to achieve the stated tension.

Tension

10 sts and 20 rows worked in garter stitch (every row K) should produce a 4in (10cm) square (but see Tension/Gauge, on page 109).

Knitting note

To avoid blocks of colour (especially if your skeins are quite different), work the garment pieces using each of the skeins in turn, knitting four or five rows from each skein in 'imaginary' stripes. If your skeins are very different, you may end up with a more stripy effect. If you want to ensure that any stripes 'match' across the back, front and sleeves, make a note of the order in which your skeins are used and the number of rows worked in each skein at each colour change.

Back

Using size 13 (9mm, old UK 00) needles cast on 40 sts. Work in garter st (every row knit) for 80 rows (16in/40cm).
Row 81: Cast off 5 sts K to end.
Row 82: Cast off 5 sts K to end.
Row 83: Cast off 5 sts K to end.
Row 84: Cast off 5 sts K to end.
Row 85: Cast off remaining 20 sts.

Front

Using size 13 (9mm, old UK 00) needles cast on 40 sts. Work in garter st (every row knit) for 60 rows (12in/30cm).
Row 61: K20 sts, turn.
Rows 62–80: Working on just these 20 sts, K rows 62–80, leaving the remaining sts on a holder or spare piece of yarn.
Row 81: Cast off 5 sts, K to end.
Row 82: K
Row 83: Cast off 5 sts, K to end.
Row 84: K
Row 85: Cast off remaining 10 sts.
With RS facing, rejoin yarn at centre of front and K to end. K20 rows.
Row 81: Cast off 5 K to end.
Row 82: K
Row 83: Cast off 5 K to end.
Row 84: K
Row 85: Cast off remaining 10 sts.

Sleeves (make two)

Using size 13 (9mm, old UK 00) needles cast on 20 sts.
Working in garter st (every row knit) increase at each end of every 5th row thus:
K2, M1 K to last 2 sts, M1, K2 until 44 sts on the needle.
Work 5 more rows g st (or as many rows as are required to achieve the desired sleeve length). Cast off.

Making up

With RS together overcast both shoulder seams. Fold one sleeve in half to find the centre of the cast off edge. With RS together place the centre of the cast off edge of the sleeve at the shoulder seam. Pin the sleeve in place, taking care to ensure that the sleeve is correctly centred at the shoulder seam. Overcast the sleeve to the main body of the garment. Repeat for the other sleeve.

With RS together backstitch the underarm and sleeve seams, working from the cuff edge of the sleeve up to the underarm and down the side seams of the main body of the garment to the cast on edge of the front/back.

Cotton Carrier Bag

This capacious and colourful bag would be great for shopping, or for carrying around your 'works in progress'. It is lined, both to give the bag more shape and to prevent small items from falling through any holes between the stitches. For a matching lining, a piece of white cotton can be used and dyed using a small amount of leftover dye (or simply lay the cotton in the bottom of the dyeing tray). You could leave yours unlined if you prefer.

I've used cotton because it doesn't stretch, is soft and pleasant to handle and can be washed easily without risk of pilling or felting. You could use a chunky or super-chunky yarn, but then be particularly careful when measuring your tension square to ensure that the yarn won't stretch out of shape in use.

The crocheted Turkish closure (see page 80) is optional; you could simply put a zip into the top of the bag lining, or use large snap fasteners, if you find that too fiddly.

The bag has a long strap, so that it can be worn across the shoulders, but you could easily adjust the number of rows worked until you reach your desired length.

Bag size

Measures approx. 11¼in (28cm) wide, 14½in (37cm) tall and 3¼in (8cm) deep; strap length is approx. 36in (90cm)

Materials and equipment for dyeing

Basic equipment listed on pages 33–6, plus:

18oz (540g) 4/2s (chunky) super American 100% cotton divided into 4 skeins of 4½oz (135g) each

18oz (540g) salt

9oz (270g) sodium carbonate

4¼gal (16.2l) water

1tsp (5ml) procion mx dye brilliant turquoise mx-g made up as below

1tsp (5ml) procion mx dye brilliant emerald mx-g made up as below

1tsp (5ml) procion mx dye lemon yellow mx-4g made up as below

Dyeing the yarn

Method

1 In a large bucket (or buckets), dissolve the salt and sodium carbonate in the water. If dyeing a piece of fabric at the same time, add a little extra salt and sodium carbonate.

2 Soak all skeins in this solution (and your lining fabric, if you are dyeing it) for at least 45 minutes.

3 While the yarn is soaking make up each of the dyes into the appropriate strength solution as stated below, following the instructions in Appendix E (see page 148):

    a 1 cup (250ml) procion mx dye brilliant turquoise at 1% solution (½tsp [2.5ml] dye and 1 cup [250ml] water)

    b 2 cups (500ml) procion mx dye brilliant turquoise at 0.25% solution (¼tsp [1.25ml] dye powder and 2 cups [500ml] water)

    c 1 cup (250ml) procion mx dye brilliant emerald at 1% solution (½tsp [2.5ml] dye and 1 cup [250ml] water)

    d 2 cups (500ml) procion mx dye brilliant emerald at 0.25% solution (¼tsp [1.25ml] dye and 2 cups [500ml] water)

    e 1 cup (250ml) procion mx dye lemon yellow at 1% solution (½tsp [2.5ml] dye and 1 cup [250ml] water)

    f 2 cups (500ml) procion mx dye lemon yellow at 0.25% solution (¼tsp [1.25ml] dye and 2 cups [500ml] water)

4 Place each of the 4 skeins in a suitable container and apply dye randomly to the yarn.

Note

Double quantities of salt and sodium carbonate were used to ensure that strong colours and good penetration of the dye were achieved with this thick yarn.

For the bag illustrated, the four different combinations below were used:

Skein 1, Green/turquoise: 0.25% emerald green (d) and 0.25% turquoise (b) were applied, with more of the emerald, to give a predominantly green colouring.

Skein 2, Yellow/green: both the 1% and 0.25% yellow solutions, (e) and (f), were applied, but only the 0.25% emerald solution (d). This ensured a predominantly yellow skein with pale green accents.

Skein 3, Turquoise/Green: the 1% turquoise (a) and 1% emerald (c) were applied, together with the 0.25% turquoise (b). Using more of the turquoise produced a predominantly turquoise skein, whilst still maintaining a green element, while using the 1% solutions created stronger colours in this skein.

Skein 4, Green/yellow: predominantly 1% emerald (c) was applied, to give a strong shade of green. To soften the effect a little, a small amount of 0.25% yellow (f) and emerald (d) were also applied.

5 As you apply the dye, gently squeeze the yarn until the dye has fully penetrated each of the skeins, turning the yarn if necessary to ensure full coverage. If the dye is not penetrating the yarn completely, or is not spreading satisfactorily, a little water can be added. Because this is a very thick yarn, it may also be necessary to spread apart the skeins to ensure that the dye has penetrated to the centre.

6 Leave the yarn to set for at least six hours. After six hours remove the yarn carefully from the container/s, rinse thoroughly and allow to dry.

To knit the bag

Material and equipment

Lining: a coordinating fabric (cotton, lightweight calico, polyester cotton or similar), cut into the following pieces:

2 pieces 12in (30cm) x 15½in (39cm)
2 pieces 4½in (11cm) wide x 22½in (56cm) long

One pair size 10 (6mm, old UK 4) needles or size required to achieve the stated tension.

Tension

12 sts and 19 rows worked in moss stitch (see below) should produce a 4in (10cm) square (but see Tension/Gauge, on page 109).

Knitting note

Work in stripes, alternating between the skeins as in pattern below.
Both sides of the bag follow the same pattern.

Pattern note

Moss stitch worked thus (over odd number of sts):
*K1, P1, rep from * to last st, K1.
This row is repeated throughout.

Work 2 pieces alike.
Using size 10 (6mm, old UK 4) needles, cast on 45 sts. Work in moss stitch (see pattern note) changing colours in the following sequence:

Sk 1	14 rows
Sk 2	10 rows
Sk 1	10 rows
Sk 3	8 rows
Sk 1	6 rows
Sk 4	5 rows

(53 rows in total). Cast off.

Gusset and strap
The gusset and strap are worked as a single piece. If you are shortening/lengthening the strap, allow 41in (102cm) for the gusset (being 11¼in [28cm] along the bottom of the bag and 15in [37cm] up each side), then add the number of inches/centimetres needed for the strap itself.

Using size 10 (6mm, old UK 4) needles, cast on 9 sts. Work in moss stitch (see pattern note), changing skeins at intervals until the piece measures 77in (192cm), or your chosen length. Cast off.

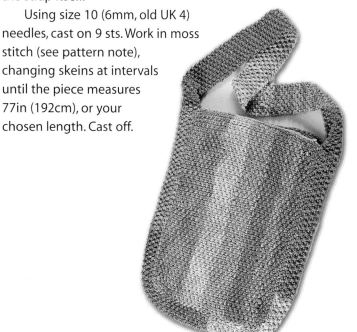

The Turkish closure

Equipment needed

Crochet hook size H (5mm)

This is based on the closure used on the saddle bags traditionally used by Turkish and Afghan nomadic peoples. These beautiful hand-woven – and often hand-dyed – bags were used historically to carry the family's belongings by camel from one encampment to another.

Method

Using size H (5mm) crochet hook, with RS of top edge of bag facing, join yarn at left-hand edge.

Make 4ch then make 28sc evenly across the top of one side of the bag (excluding the gusset). Fasten off.

Turn the bag so that the RS is facing. Join yarn at the left-hand edge and make 1ch.

Sl st 28 sts evenly across the top edge of this side of the bag.

Turn. * Make 14ch, then sl st into base st of ch. 4sl st. ** Repeat from * to ** 5 more times, make 14ch. sl st into base of ch, 2sl st, make 14ch. Fasten off.

Using a Turkish closure

To close the bag, start at the end opposite the loose chain with the tassel.

1 Pass the first loop through the row of double crochet.

2 Pass the second loop through the nearest double crochet.

3 Pass the second loop through the first loop and draw closed to form the beginning of a kind of chain.

4 Pass the third loop through the nearest double crochet.

5 Pass the third loop through the second loop as at 3.

6 Continue in this way, passing each new loop through the row of double crochet then through the preceding loop. The loops, when tightened, should form what looks like a row of chain stitches.

7 When you reach the final loop, pass the loose chain with the tassel through the double crochet and through the last loop to completely close the bag.

7.1

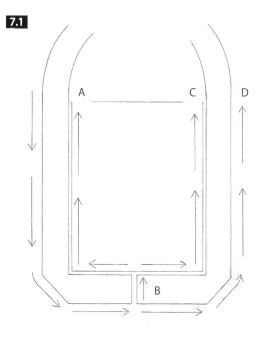

Leave the lining bag with its RS tog and snip the corners carefully, to avoid cutting across the stitched seams. Press open all seams. Place the lining, RS still tog, inside the knitted bag. Turn in the top edge of the lining and pin in place just below the crocheted edge, being sure to align the side seams and gussets. Press over the work carefully with a damp cloth, so as not to flatten the knitting too much. To attach the lining, slip stitch by hand around the top of the bag to form a neat edge. Add a zip, or the Turkish closure described above.

Tassel

To complete the bag, make a tassel in your dyed cotton yarn according to the instructions on page 132, and attach to the loose end of chain on the closure.

Making up

Place one end of the gusset/strap piece halfway along one of the short edges of one of the main body pieces (see Fig 7.1, above). With RS tog, overcast the strip to the main body piece, starting at the centre of the short side, around the corner and up the long side of the main piece to the top edge (A). Place the other end of the strip next to the first end. With RS tog, overcast the two ends tog (B) then overcast along the short side and up the long side of the main body piece to the top edge (C). Place RS of the other main body piece and the other side of the strip together and overcast the two tog starting from the top edge, working down across the short side, round the corner and up to the top edge (D).

Lining

Make a bag shape from the lining fabric, following the steps for the bag (above), but using a backstitch or sewing machine seam and leaving a 1in (2.5cm) seam allowance instead of overcasting. The strap is not lined so the gusset piece will stop at the top of the bag.

Crochet Projects

Ultrawarm
Chenille Scarf

Scarf size

Approx. 80in long x 6½in wide (2m x 17cm)

Materials and equipment for dyeing

Basic equipment listed on pp. 33–6, plus:

18oz (540g) coarse viscose cotton
   chenille yarn divided into 4 skeins of
   4½oz (135g) each

9oz (270g) salt

4½oz (135g) sodium carbonate

4¼gal (16.2l) water

½tsp (2.5ml) procion mx dye lemon
   yellow mx-4g made up into a 1%
   solution (½tsp [2.5ml] dye and 1 cup
   [250ml] water)

½tsp (2.5ml) procion mx dye brilliant
   emerald mx-g made up into a 1%
   solution (½tsp [2.5ml] dye and 1 cup
   [250ml] water)

This project is fantastically quick and easy to make but looks a million dollars. Whether you prefer rich colours or pastels, the effect is equally stunning. The fluffiness of the chenille also traps lots of air, making it a lovely warm and practical addition to your wardrobe. Working into the space between the stitches rather than into the top of each stitch gives the scarf a ridged effect, enhancing its texture.

The length of the scarf can be adjusted easily by increasing or decreasing the number of stitches, and you can work more or fewer rows to adjust the width of the scarf if required. This scarf also lends itself well to experimenting with different yarns, since the overall size is not critical and there is no shaping to worry about. You could, of course, add some large beads if you want a more flamboyant look, or even a fringe.

Dyeing the yarn

Method

1 In a large bucket, dissolve the salt and sodium carbonate in the water, and soak all four skeins for at least 45 minutes in this solution.

2 While the yarn is soaking, make up the two dyes into a 1% strength stock solution using ½tsp (2.5ml) dye and 1 cup (250ml) water for each colour, following the instructions in Appendix E (page 148). Mark the bottles at the 1 cup (250ml) line, with a pen or sticky tape.
   Dye all four skeins in the same way, either in two separate containers (such as large cat litter trays) or four smaller containers, to allow the dye to penetrate the yarn thoroughly. Use a progressively dilute solution of the original two dyes, to produce a range of colours from deep yellow to mid-lemon, and deep bright green to mid-green, respectively. Shades of turquoise will be produced where the two colours blend together. Squeeze the yarn and add water to ensure that the colours are well blended, to give a more subtle, harmonious effect.

3 Skeins 1–4: with 1 cup (250ml) of each of the two dyes in a 1% solution, apply roughly one quarter of each dye in stripes across the yarn. Turn the yarn over and repeat, leaving roughly half the original amount of each of the dyes.

4 Top up the two dyes with cold water back to the 1 cup (250ml) line, so that they are half the original strength. Apply a quarter of each colour, again in stripes across the yarn. Turn the yarn and repeat the process.

5 Again top up the dyes with cold water to the 1 cup (250ml) line, to make dye approximately a quarter of its original strength. Apply a quarter of each of these paler dye solutions in stripes. Turn and apply a further quarter of each of the two solutions in stripes across the yarns.

6 Top each of the dye solutions up to the 1 cup (250ml) line one final time. Apply the remaining dye to the yarn in stripes as before, turning the yarn halfway through the process.

7 Gently squeeze the yarn until the dye has fully penetrated each of the skeins, turning if necessary, to ensure full coverage. If the dye isn't penetrating the yarn satisfactorily, add a little water and, if necessary, separate the skeins, so that the dye can penetrate to the centre.

8 Leave the yarn to set for at least six hours, then remove it carefully from the container/s, rinse thoroughly and allow to dry.

To crochet the scarf

Equipment

One size K (UK 7mm) crochet hook.

Tension

7 sts and 3 rows worked in dtr into lp (see below) should produce a 4in (10cm) square (but see Tension/Gauge, on page 109).

Pattern note

Dtr (UK trtr) worked thus:
Yrh 3 times. Insert hook into next st, yrh and draw back through (5 lps on hook). *Yrh pull through 2 lps*. Rep from * to * 3 more times (4 times in total). 1 lp remains on the hook.
   Make 134ch. Miss the first 4ch and work a dtr into the 5th ch from the hook. Work a dtr into each ch to end. **Turn and work 4ch. Work a dtr into each lp (i.e. into the large space between the stitches rather than just under the top of the stitch as would normally be the case) to end**. Repeat from ** to ** three more times (5 rows in total).
Fasten off.

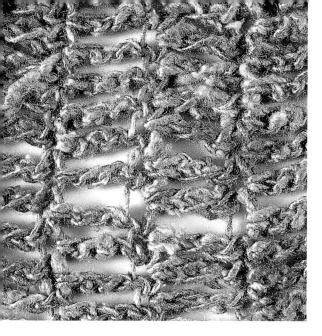

Sleeveless Top, in Wild Thai Silk

Silk is a good all-weather fibre, as it is warm when the weather is cool, but allows the skin to breathe if the temperature rises. The naturally camel-coloured Thai silk used here has slubs and a slight lustre which make it really special, and the natural colour mutes the otherwise bright dyes, producing attractive, subtle shades. This top is flattering to the fuller figure, as the silk has a lovely drape.

To create the light, open texture, the top is crocheted mostly in an unusual stitch, based broadly on a double treble, with a small amount of single and double crochet for the shaping. It is worked sideways from top to bottom in a single piece, so there are no side seams to join, only a small amount of stitching at the shoulders and sewing in a couple of ends. There are no fastenings, but you could add tie fastenings if you wished.

The size of the top
To fit a 34–36in (86–92cm) bust

Materials and equipment for dyeing
Basic equipment listed on pages 33–6, plus:

8oz (240g) 100% Thai silk yarn divided into 3 skeins of approximately 2½oz (80g) each

4oz (120g) salt

2oz (60g) sodium carbonate

1¾gal (7.2l) water

½tsp (2.5ml) procion mx dye lemon yellow mx-4g

½tsp (2.5ml) procion mx dye deep purple mx-1

½tsp (2.5ml) procion mx dye cerulean blue mx-g

3 jars/bottles, each capable of holding 2 cups (500ml) dye solution

Dyeing the yarn

Dyeing method

1 In a large bucket, dissolve the salt and sodium carbonate in the water (if using several small buckets, divide the salt, water and sodium carbonate equally between the buckets). Soak all the skeins in this solution for at least 45 minutes.

2 While the yarn is soaking, make up each of the dyes into the appropriate strength solution as stated below, following the instructions in Appendix E (see page 148). Make up 2 cups (500ml) of each of the yellow, purple and blue dyes into 0.5 % solutions in separate bottles (½tsp [2.5ml] dye and 2 cups [500ml] water in each one).

3 Take three dishes and place one skein in each, arranging the yarn in a random fashion, then apply the three dye solutions randomly to the skeins, using approximately the same amount of each dye in each dish. It is not necessary to use all of each of the solutions so, once the dyes have been applied and you are happy with the result, simply leave to set for six hours.

4 Once the yarn has set, remove carefully from the container, rinse thoroughly and allow to dry.

The dye can make the Thai silk a little stiff. It will soften as it is crocheted, but you may wish to add some fabric softener when rinsing.

Tip

To crochet the top

Equipment

One size I (5.5mm) and one size J (6mm) crochet hook, or sizes required to achieve the stated tension.

Tension

Using a size I (5.5mm) hook, 12 sts and 5 rows worked in long st (see below) should produce a 4in (10cm) square (see Tension/Gauge, page 109).

Pattern note – 'Long stitch'

On a base of chain, work into 4th ch from hook and make a 'long st' thus:
Yrh, draw through lp (3 lps on hook)
Yrh draw through 1 lp (3 lps on hook)
Yrh draw through 1 lp (3 lps on hook)
Yrh draw through 2 lps (2 lps remaining)
Yrh draw through remaining 2 lps (1 lp remains on hook)

Using a hook one size larger than the size needed to achieve the stated tension (i.e. size J), make 50ch. Change to size I hook and work as follows:

Row 1: Miss first 3ch, work into 4th ch from hook and 'long st' (see pattern note) to end of row (47 sts including the st made by the 3ch)
Row 2: 3ch, make 2 long st, work twice in long st into next st (to increase 1 st), work long st to end (48 sts).
Row 3: 3ch, work long st to last 3 st, work twice in long st into next st, work long st to end (49 sts).
Row 4: As row 2 (50 sts).
Row 5: As row 3 (51 sts).

Shape neck
At the end of row 5 make 11ch.
Row 6: Miss first 3ch work long st into 4th ch and work long st to end (58 sts).
Row 7: 3ch, long st to end.

Row 8: 3ch, work next st in long st until 2 lps remain on hook. Work long st into next st until 3 lps remain in total. Yrh draw through all 3 lps (decreasing 1 st). Long st to end (57 sts).
Row 9: 3ch, long st to end.

Shape armhole
Row 10: Sl st 18 sts, make 3ch and work in long st to end (39sts).
Row 11: 3ch, long st to end.
Row 12: 3ch, long st to end.
Row 13: 3ch, 19 long st, 11dc, 8sc (39 sts including the st made by the 3ch).

Shape underarm
Row 14: 2ch, 7sc, 11dc, 20 long st (39 sts including the st made by the 2ch).
Row 15: 3ch, long st to end.
Row 16: 3ch, long st to end.
Row 17: 3ch, long st to end.

Shape armhole
At end of row 17 make 22ch.
Row 18: Work into 4th ch, long st to end (57 sts).
Row 19: 3ch, long st to end.
Row 20: 3ch, work long st twice into next st, long st to end (58 sts).
Rows 21–25: 3ch, long st to end.

Shape centre back dart
Row 26: 2ch, 9sc, 15dc, 33 long st (58 sts including st made by 2ch).
Row 27: 3ch, 32 long st, 15dc, 10sc (58 sts including st made by 3ch).
Rows 28–33: 3ch, long st to end.
Row 34: 3 ch, work 2 long st, work long st into next st until 2 lps remain. Work long st into next st until 3 lps remain on the hook in total. Yrh, draw through all 3 lps (1 st decreased). Long st to end. (57 sts).
Row 35: 3ch, long st to end.

Shape armhole
Row 36: Sl st 18 sts. Make 3ch, long st to end (39 sts including st made by 3ch).
Rows 37–38: 3ch. Long st to end.

Shape underarm
Row 39: 3ch, 19 long st, 11dc, 8sc (39 sts including the st made by the 3ch).
Row 40: 2ch, 7sc, 11dc, 20 long st (39 sts including the st made by the 2ch).
Row 41–43: 3ch. Long st to end.

Shape armhole
At end of row 43 make 22ch.
Row 44: Miss 1st 3ch, work into 4th ch and long st to end (57 sts including st made by 3 ch).
Row 45: 3ch, long st to end.
Row 46: 3ch, make 2 long st, work twice in long st into next st (to increase 1 st), work long st to end (58 sts).
Row 47: 3ch. Long st to end.

Shape neck
Row 48: Sl st 8 sts. Make 3ch. Long st to end (51 sts including st made by 3ch).
Row 49: Work long st to last 4 sts. Work long st into next st until 2 lps remain. Work long st into next st until 3 lps remain on the hook in total. Yrh, draw through all 3 lps (1 st decreased). Long st last 2 sts. (50 sts).
Row 50: Work 2 long st, work long st into next st until 2 lps remain. Work long st into next st until 3 lps remain on the hook in total. Yrh, draw through all 3 lps (1 st decreased). Long st to end (49 sts).
Row 51: Work long st to last 4 sts. Work long st into next st until 2 lps remain. Work long st into next st until 3 lps remain on the hook in total. Yrh, draw through all 3 lps (1 st decreased). Long st last 2 sts. (48 sts).
Row 52: Work 2 long st, work long st into next st until 2 lps remain. Work long st into next st until 3 lps remain on the hook in total. Yrh, draw through all 3 lps (1 st decreased). Long st to end (47 sts).
Fasten off.

Making up

With RS tog, carefully overcast the shoulder seams. Darn in any ends.

Beaded Wrist Purse

This stunning little purse is quite simple and quick to make and the beads add a glamorous dimension, although you could leave them off if you prefer. It is best to dye the yarn before purchasing the beads, as you can then take a sample piece to the shop to help you get a good colour match.

The Lurex in the yarn does not accept the dye, which is why you can still see green and gold-coloured sparkles in the finished bag. If you want a more subtle look, a tubular-type yarn or a cotton yarn of a similar weight would look effective.

Size of purse
Approx. 3in (7.5cm) across the base, and 3½in (9cm) tall

Materials and equipment for dyeing
Basic equipment listed on pages 33–6, plus:

1oz (30g) 80% viscose/20% Lurex 'glitter' tube yarn (4ply)

½oz (15g) salt

¼oz (7.5g) sodium carbonate

¼gal (0.9l) water

¼tsp (1.25ml) procion mx dye deep purple mx-1 made up into a 1% solution (¼tsp [1.25ml] dye and ½ cup [125ml] water)

¼tsp (1.25ml) procion mx dye black mx-k made up into a 1% solution (¼tsp [1.25ml] dye and ½ cup [125ml] water)

Large piece of clingfilm

Dyeing the yarn

Dyeing note

For such a small item it is difficult to give meaningful quantities of dye solution, so I have given a volume of solution which will be much more than you will need, but is easy to measure.

Dyeing method

1 Dissolve the salt and sodium carbonate in the water in a bucket and soak the yarn for at least 45 minutes in this solution.

2 While the yarn is soaking make up each of the dyes into the appropriate strength solution as stated above, following the instructions in Appendix E (see page 148).

3 Place the skein on the clingfilm, folded in half in a horseshoe-shape, and apply dye in broad stripes across the yarn. (N.B. I only used about a quarter of the dye solution, as the yarn took the dye very quickly, so I recommend applying the dye solution slowly and carefully to avoid lots of excess dye swilling around on the clingfilm.)

4 Fold the clingfilm carefully to enclose the yarn and leave for at least six hours to set, then remove the yarn carefully from the film, rinse thoroughly and allow to dry.

To crochet the purse

Equipment

One size F (4mm) crochet hook or size required to achieve the stated tension
305 beads (300 for the design with five spares)

Tension

19 sts and 16 rows worked flat in sc (UK dc) should produce a 10cm (4in) square (but see Tension/Gauge, page 109).

Thread 300 beads onto the yarn (see page 135). Using size F (4mm) hook, make 3ch and sl st into first ch to form a circle.
Round 1: Work 6sc into centre of circle.
Round 2: Work 2sc into each of 6sc from previous round (12 sts).
Round 3: *sc, 2sc into next st.** rep. from * to ** 5 more times (18 sts).
The next round (4) is the first of the bead rounds:
Round 4: *sc, sc, 2sc into next st**. Rep from * to ** 5 more times BUT where 2sc are worked into the same st, push up 5 beads between the 1st and 2nd sc (so, sc, sc, sc, push up 5 beads, sc into same st) (24 sts).
Round 5: *sc, sc, sc, 2sc into same st**. Rep from * to ** 5 more times (30 sts).
Round 6: *sc, sc, sc, sc, 2sc into same st**. Rep from * to ** 5 more times (36 sts).
Round 7: *sc, push up 15 beads, sc, sc, push up 15 beads, sc, sc, push up 15 beads, 2sc into same st**. Rep 5 more times (18 sets of beads, 42 sts).
Round 8: Work hdc into each st.
Round 9: As row 8 BUT pushing up 1 bead in between each st.
Rounds 10–12: Work hdc into each st.
Round 13: As row 8 BUT pushing up 5 beads between each hdc.
Rounds 14–16: Work hdc into each st.
Round 17: dc into each st.
Round 18: sc into each st.
Fasten off.

> **Tip**
>
> *If the yarn becomes twisted as you work, use a safety pin, small bulldog clip or lightweight clothes peg to clip your work below the crochet hook and prevent the stitches from unravelling. Then carefully remove the crochet hook, making sure you know where you are up to in the pattern. Hold up the yarn ball with the beads on in one hand and dangle the work loosely. The work should spin gently until the yarn unwinds (you can assist this with your other hand). Once the excess twist has unwound, replace the crochet hook, unclip the yarn and continue where you left off.*

Making up

Make a drawstring by working a piece of chain approx. 15in (38cm) long. Work 1 row sc, fasten off, leaving an end of approx. 5in (13cm). Taking your piece of chain, weave it through the row of double crochet. Use the long tail to slip stitch into the starting chain and fasten off, weaving the end in securely before cutting off neatly.

Elegant Evening Bag

This delightful little evening bag would work equally well as a bag for wedding favours, as weddings are occasions when a hand-made gift is truly treasured, and gifts are commonly given to bridesmaids as a reminder of their part in the special event. You could make a set in colours to coordinate with the wedding flowers or the bridesmaids' dresses; or, by making a number of skeins in similar shades, you could make a lovely set of gift bags, and fill them with sweets, jewellery, or other small keepsakes.

The yarn I have used gives quite a firm-textured fabric but, if you want the bag to stand on its own without collapsing, you could insert a small tube of cardboard when needed. The drawstring is an easy-to-make closure, enabling the bags to be worn on the wrist, if desired.

As with the previous project, I recommend dyeing your yarn before purchasing the beads, taking care to choose beads with large enough holes to accommodate the yarn.

The beads can, of course, be omitted if you prefer and, if you would like a more glitzy effect, substitute the plain viscose yarn for a viscose/Lurex mix.

Bag size
Approx. 3in (7.5cm) across the base, 3½in (9cm) tall

Materials and equipment for dyeing
Basic equipment listed on pages 33–6, plus:

1oz (30g) viscose ribbon tube yarn (4ply)

½oz (15g) salt

¼oz (7.5g) sodium carbonate

¼gal (0.9l) water

¼tsp (1.25ml) procion mx dye scarlet mx-3g made up into a 0.25% solution (¼tsp [1.25ml] dye and 2 cups [500ml] water)

¼tsp (1.25ml) procion mx dye cerulean blue mx-g made up into a 0.25% solution (¼tsp [1.25ml] dye and 2 cups [500ml] water)

Large piece of clingfilm

Dyeing the yarn

Dyeing notes

As with the purse on page 90, for such a small object it is difficult to give meaningful quantities of dye solution. I have, therefore, given a volume of solution which will be considerably more than you should need, but is easy to measure.

Method

1 Dissolve the salt and sodium carbonate in the water in a bucket and soak the yarn in this solution for at least 45 minutes.

2 While the yarn is soaking make up each of the dyes into the appropriate strength solution as stated above, following the instructions in Appendix E (see page 148).

3 Place the skein on the clingfilm, fold it in half in a horseshoe-shape and apply dye slowly, in a random fashion across the yarn. To ensure that no areas of pure red are left in the final piece, apply blue over red, red over blue, and so on. Leave pure blue areas, however, to give blue highlights in the finished yarn. N.B. The yarn takes the dye very quickly, so apply the dye solution slowly and carefully to avoid excess dye swilling around on the clingfilm.

4 Fold the clingfilm carefully to enclose the yarn and leave for at least six hours to set, then remove the yarn carefully from the film, rinse it thoroughly and allow to dry.

To crochet the bag

Equipment

One size F (4mm) crochet hook or size required to achieve the stated tension
90 beads: 84 for the design with six spares
39in (1m) ribbon for the drawstring

Tension

20 sts and 5 rows worked flat in sc should produce a 4in (10cm) square (but see Tension/Gauge, page 109).

Begin by threading 84 beads onto the yarn using the instructions on page 135.
Using size F (4mm) hook, make 3ch and sl st the 3ch tog to form a circle.
Round 1: Work 6sc into centre of circle.
Round 2: Work 2sc into each of 6sc from previous round (12sts).
Round 3: *sc, 2sc into next st**. Rep from * to ** 5 more times (18sts).
Round 4: *sc, sc, 2sc into next st**. Rep from * to ** 5 more times (24sts).
Round 5: *sc, sc, sc, 2sc into same st**. Rep from * to ** 5 more times (30sts).
Round 6: *sc, sc, sc, sc, 2sc into same st**. Rep from * to ** 5 more times (36sts).
Round 7: *sc, sc, sc, sc, sc, 2sc into same st** Rep from * to ** 5 more times (42 sts).
Round 8: Mark the start of the round with a spare piece of thread and work sc in each st. The next round is the first of the bead rounds.
Round 9: *push up 1 bead, sc**. Rep from * to ** 5 more times, ending with a sc, sc (21 beads added).
Round 10: *push up 1 bead, sc **. Rep from * to ** until 21 more beads added (42 in total over the two rounds).
Rounds 11–24: sc
Round 25: As round 9.
Round 26: As round 10.
Round 27: dc
Round 28: sc
Fasten off.

Making up

Taking your piece of ribbon, thread it through the row of double crochet to form a double drawstring, as illustrated on pages 133–4.

Sunhat in Textured Bouclé Cotton

Hat size

To fit a child aged approximately 5–15 years

Finished size: head circumference approx. 21½ in (55cm)

Materials and equipment for dyeing

Basic equipment listed on pp. 33–6, plus:

8oz (240g) 100% cotton gimp ordinary twist divided into 2 skeins

4oz (120g) salt

2oz (60g) sodium carbonate

1¾gal (7.2l) water

½tsp (2.5ml) procion mx dye orange-scarlet mx-g made up into a 1% solution (½tsp [2.5ml] dye and 1 cup [250ml] water)

½tsp (2.5ml) procion mx dye royal blue mx-r made up into a 1% solution (½tsp [2.5ml] dye and 1 cup [250ml] water)

½tsp (2.5ml) procion mx dye lemon yellow mx-4g made up into a 1% solution (½tsp [2.5ml] dye and 1 cup [250ml] water)

Large piece of clingfilm

This delightful hat is relatively easy to make, and the yarn used is firm, but has enough 'give' to accommodate a good range of sizes. The rainbow colours would brighten up any summer outfit, but pastel-coloured yarn would look very attractive, too.

The hat has an upfolded brim and is trimmed with a flower crocheted in the same yarn but, if you prefer, you could leave the flower out altogether, or buy a toning sew-on one from a haberdashery store.

Dyeing the yarn

Method

1 Dissolve the salt and sodium carbonate in the water in a bucket and soak the yarn in this solution for at least 45 minutes.

2 While the yarn is soaking, make up each of the dyes into the appropriate strength solution as stated above, following the instructions in Appendix E (see page 148).

3 Place the skein on the clingfilm, folded in half in a horseshoe-shape, and apply the dye in broadly equal stripes across the yarn in the order specified below. Make sure you leave an equal amount of space undyed between each stripe at this stage, as this will be the area which will be blended to form the intermediate colours, orange, green and violet/purple.

4 Work in the following order from left to right:

Yellow, scarlet, blue, yellow. Once you have applied the pure colours, fill in the undyed areas by using combinations of the dyes as follows (again working from left to right):

Yellow/scarlet (apply the yellow first as the scarlet is stronger and you may need more yellow than scarlet), to give orange

Scarlet/blue in broadly equal amounts, to give violet/purple

Yellow/blue (again apply the yellow first, more than the blue, as the blue is a strong colour), to provide the green

5 Squeeze the yarn gently to blend the neighbouring colours into one another, adding more dye if required. Gently lift the yarn to check that the dye has penetrated all the yarn; if not, turn the yarn over very

Tip

A couple of pieces of kitchen paper, placed on the clingfilm under the yarn, will prevent stray dye swilling around under the yarn and muddying the colours on the underside.

carefully, ensuring that you turn the short distance across the yarn, and not lengthwise from one end to the other, otherwise your colours will get mixed up.

6 Fold the clingfilm carefully to enclose the yarn; leave for at least six hours to set, then remove the yarn carefully from the film, rinse thoroughly and allow to dry.

To crochet the hat

Equipment

One each of size H (5mm) and size G (4.5mm) crochet hooks or sizes required to achieve the stated tension for the hat.

Tension

12 sts and 12 rows worked flat in sc using size H (5mm) hook should produce a 4in (10cm) square (but see Tension/Gauge, page 109).

Using a size H (5mm) hook, make 3ch and join with a sl st.
Round 1: Work 6sc into the centre of the circle formed by the 3 joined ch. Mark the start of the round with a small piece of scrap yarn and continue working in rounds as follows:
Round 2: 2sc into each of 6sc from previous round (12 sts).
Round 3: *sc, 2sc **. Rep from * to ** 5 more times (18 sts).
Round 4: *sc, sc, 2sc **. Rep from * to ** 5 more times (24 sts).
Round 5: *sc, sc, sc, 2sc **. Rep from * to ** 5 more times (30 sts).

Round 6: *sc, sc, sc, sc, 2sc **. Rep from * to ** 5 more times (36 sts).

Round 7: *sc, sc, sc, sc, sc, 2sc **. Rep from * to ** 5 more times (42 sts).

Round 8: *sc, sc, sc, sc, sc, sc, 2sc **. Rep from * to ** 5 more times (48 sts.)

Round 9: sc

Round 10: *sc, sc, sc, sc, sc, sc, sc, 2sc **. Rep from * to ** 5 more times (54 sts).

Round 11: sc

Round 12: *sc, sc, sc, sc, sc, sc, sc, sc, 2sc **. Rep from * to ** 5 more times (60 sts) (you should have 8sc between each 2sc, with 60 sts in total).

Rounds 13–24: sc

Shape brim

Round 25: *sc, 2sc **. Rep from * to ** to end of round (as marked by the piece of spare yarn).

Round 26: sc

Round 27: *2sc, sc, sc, sc**. Rep from * to ** to end of round.

Round 28: sc

Round 29: sc. Sl st last st to first st of the round and fasten off.

Flower (optional)

With a size G (4.5 mm) hook make 6ch and sl st chain into a circle. Working into centre of circle work * sc, 3dc, sc **. Rep from * to ** 4 more times to form the petals. Sl st the final sc to the first sc, then fasten off.

Flower centre

Make 4ch and sl st chain into a circle. Work 6sc into centre of circle. Sl st final st to the first and fasten off.

Making up

Hat

Fold up a flap at the front of the hat and stitch in place with a couple of small stitches if required.

Flower

Place the flower centre over the centre of the petals to completely cover the centre hole and stitch carefully in place. Stitch the completed flower onto the centre of the upturned flap at the front of the hat.

12

Mobile
Phone Holster

Holster size

To fit an average-size mobile phone
approx. 5½ in (14cm) long

Materials and equipment for dyeing

Basic equipment listed on pages 33–6, plus:

1½ oz (45g) 2.5s (4ply) viscose/cotton slub

¾ oz (22.5g) salt

½ oz (15g) sodium carbonate

⅓ gal (1.35l) water

½ tsp (2.5ml) procion mx dye orange-
scarlet mx-g made up into a 1%
solution (½ tsp [2.5ml] dye and 1 cup
[250ml] water)

½ tsp (2.5ml) procion mx dye royal blue
mx-r made up into a 1% solution
(½ tsp [2.5ml] dye and 1 cup [250ml]
water)

½ tsp (2.5ml) procion mx dye lemon
yellow mx-4g made up into a 1%
solution (½ tsp [2.5ml] dye and 1 cup
[250ml] water)

Large piece of clingfilm

*If your mobile phone ever gets lost at the
bottom of your bag, this is the project for
you, as it will keep your phone to hand.*

*The holster can be made any length you
wish, to accommodate the seemingly ever-
changing size of mobile phones. The strap
can also be made to whatever length suits
you, whether over-the-shoulder, across-the-
shoulder, round the neck, or belt style. The
holster is fastened with a drawstring, but a
strip of hook-and-loop tape, a small button,
or a snap-fastener would be equally practical.*

*You don't need much yarn, so this is a
great project for using up remnants. I have
used a cotton viscose, because it takes dye
well and the viscose gives a slight lustre which
is subtle but effective, but it would also work
well with a plain, fine cotton, a slubby cotton
or a fine wool. Beware of anything too fluffy
or hairy, though, as you don't want fluff
all over your keypad.*

Dyeing the yarn

Method

1 Dissolve the salt and sodium carbonate in the water in a bucket and soak the yarn in this solution for at least 45 minutes.

2 While the yarn is soaking, make up each of the dyes into the appropriate strength solution as stated above, following the instructions in Appendix E (see page 148).

3 Place the skein on the clingfilm, folded in half in a horseshoe-shape, and apply the dye carefully, in roughly equal stripes across the yarn in the order specified below. Make sure you leave an equal amount of space undyed between each stripe at this stage, as this will be the area which will be blended to form the intermediate colours, orange, green and violet/purple.

4 Work in the following order from left to right:

   Yellow, scarlet, blue, yellow. Once you have applied the pure colours, fill in the undyed areas by using combinations of the dyes as follows (again working from left to right):

   Yellow/scarlet (apply the yellow first as the scarlet is stronger and you may need more yellow than scarlet), to give orange

   Scarlet/blue in broadly equal amounts, to give violet/purple

   Yellow/blue (again apply the yellow first, more than the blue, as the blue is a strong colour), to provide the green.

5 Squeeze the yarn gently to blend the neighbouring colours into one another, adding more dye if required. Gently lift the yarn to check that the dye has penetrated all the yarn. If not, you can turn the yarn if you are very careful, but make sure you turn the short distance sideways and not lengthwise from one end to the other, as otherwise your colours will get mixed up.

6 Fold the clingfilm carefully to enclose the yarn and leave for at least six hours to set, then remove the yarn carefully from the film, rinse thoroughly and allow to dry.

To crochet the holster

Equipment

One size E (3.5mm) crochet hook or size required to achieve the stated tension.

Tension

20 sts and 24 rows worked flat in sc using a size E hook should produce a 4in (10cm) square (but see Tension/Gauge, on page 109).

Using size E (3.5mm) hook (or the size required to achieve the stated tension), make 3ch.
Sl st the 3ch tog to form a circle.
Round 1: Work 6sc into centre of circle.
Round 2: Work 2sc into each of 6dc from previous round (12 sts).
Round 3: *sc, 2sc into next st**. Rep from * to ** 5 more times (18 sts).
Round 4: *sc, sc, 2sc into next st**. Rep from * to ** 5 more times, (24 sts).
Round 5: *sc, sc, sc, 2sc into same st**. Rep from * to ** 5 more times (30 sts).
Round 6 onwards: cont in sc until tube measures to the top of the phone.
Next round: dc into each st until a full round of dc has been completed
Sl st final dc to first st and fasten off.

Drawstring
Make a length of ch approx. 10in (26cm). Sc into each ch and fasten off.

Strap

Make a length of ch 37½in (95cm) long
(or desired length).

Row 1: sc

Row 2: sc

Fasten off.

Making up

Weave the drawstring in and out of the row of
double crochet stitches at the top of the tube
and, following the instructions for a simple
drawstring on page 133, leave the ends equal
and meeting in the centre. Attach the strap to
the back of the holster as shown in Fig 8.1
(above), slip stitching neatly in place.

Fig 8.1 Attaching the strap

\ = slip stitch

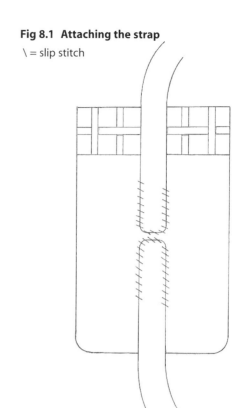

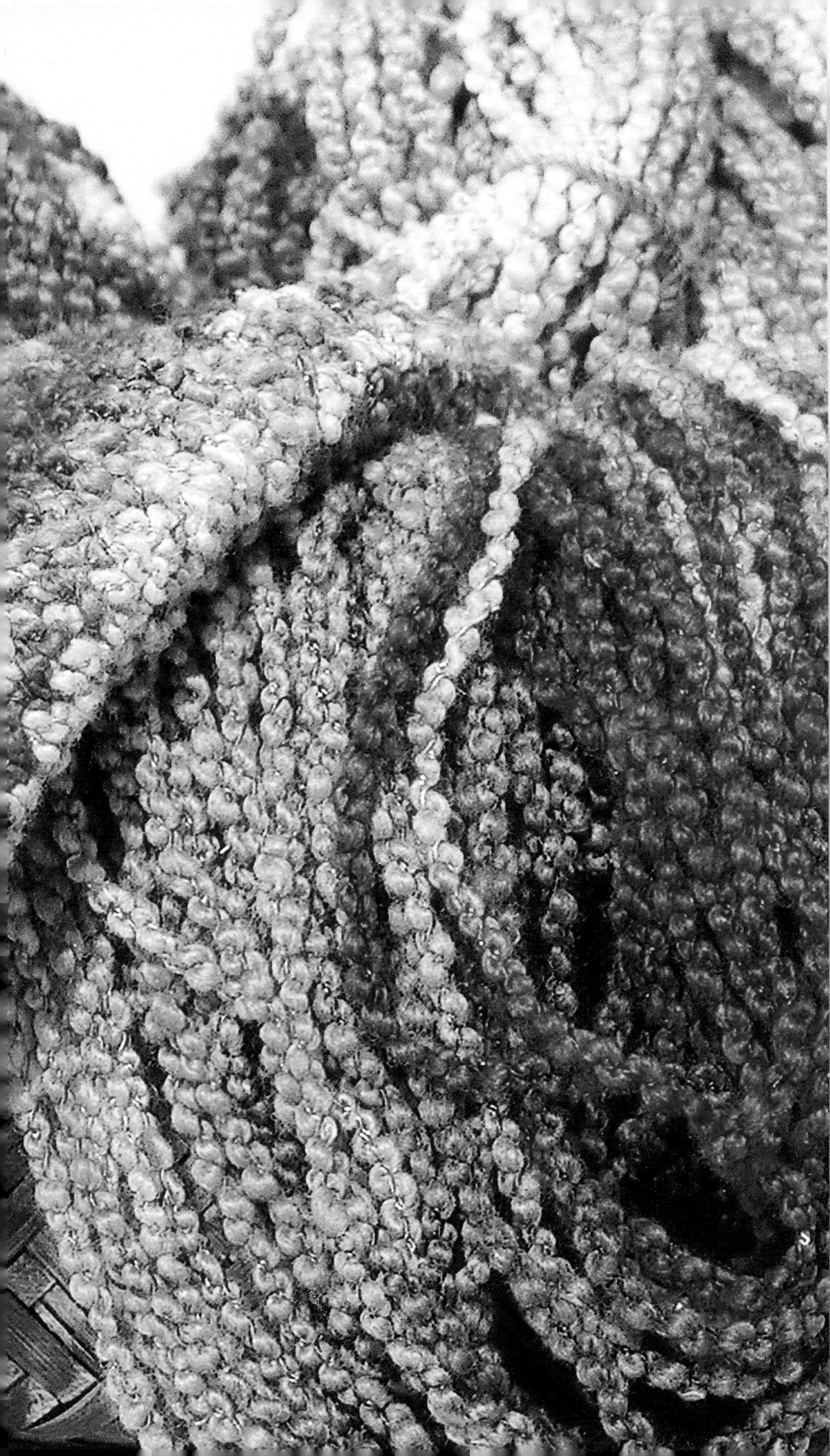

Back to Basics

Understanding Pattern Instructions

Abbreviations used in the text

Patterns are heavily abbreviated to make them short and easier to print. The abbreviations may seem unfamiliar but, with practice, they will become second nature. It may be useful to take a photocopy of this page, to refer to until you become familiar with the terms.

approx.	approximately	oz	ounce/s
beg	beginning	p	purl
ch	chain/chain stitches	p2tog	purl 2 stitches together
cm	centimetres	rem	remain(s/ing)
cont	continue(s/d)	rep	repeat
dc	double crochet	RS	right side
dec	decrease(s)	rnd	round(s)
dtr	double treble	sl	slip
fl oz	fluid ounce(s)	sl st	slip stitch(es)
g	gram(s)	st(s)	stitch(es)
gal	gallon(s)	st st	stocking stitch (knit one row,
gs	garter stitch (every row knit)		purl one row)
htr	half treble	tbsp	tablespoon
in	inch(es)	tog	together
inc	increase(s)	tr	treble
k	knit	trtr	treble treble
kg	kilogram(s)	tsp	teaspoon (5ml)
k2tog	knit 2 stitches together	WS	wrong side
lp(s)	loop(s)	yd	yard(s)
m1	make 1	yfwd	yarn forward (bring yarn to the
m	metres		front of the work)

Format

The patterns follow the same format, with materials and equipment first, then any special instructions for that pattern, followed by the knitting or crochet instructions, and finally advice on making up the pieces.

Where items are made in several pieces, each piece will have its own instructions. It is best to make the pieces in the order specified in the pattern, since later sections may ask you to repeat sections from earlier pieces (for example, a front will commonly say 'work as for back to ....').

Repeats and asterisks

Where a pattern has a repeat this is normally indicated by asterisks. So, if a pattern tells you to work *K1, P1 **, rep from * to **, this means that you should knit one stitch, purl one stitch, knit one stitch, purl one stitch, either for as many repeats as specified or to the end of the row.

Read a section of a pattern at a time. Sometimes, particularly with necklines and shoulder shaping, you may have two sets of decreases/increases going on at once. If you only read the first part of a sentence, you may miss the second set of adjustments/ measurements and have to rip back your work when you realize you have missed them.

Tension/Gauge

Not everyone knits or crochets to exactly the same proportions. For this reason, patterns will ask you to make a tension square/swatch (or gauge swatch) before you begin, and will specify which stitch and size of needles/hook to use. The purpose of the tension square is to ensure that the piece turns out the same size as that specified in the pattern.

Whilst tension is only measured over 4in (10cm), a larger square is normally worked to allow for distortions in both the cast on and cast off rows, and at the edges. Patterns will therefore give the number of stitches/rows measured over 4in (10cm), but it is advisable to work a square at least 8in (20cm), cast it off and press it, then measure the tension over a 4in (10cm) square in the centre of the larger square you have made.

If your tension doesn't match that specified in the pattern, and there are too many stitches/rows in your square, increase the needle/hook size; if there are too few stitches/rows in your square, decrease the size of needles/hook.

If you cannot get both the rows and the stitches per inch/cm correct, go for the correct stitches and use measurements to adjust the rows rather than relying purely on the number of rows. For example, if a pattern calls for 20sts and 18 rows to 4in (10cm) using size 6 (4mm, old UK 8) and you have 20sts and 20 rows with this size of needles, and 18sts and 18 rows with the next size down, use the size 6 (4mm, old UK 8) needles which give the correct stitch measurement. You may need to adjust the number of rows being worked, relying on length measurements rather than counting rows and the proportions at the neckline may not be exactly as specified, but you should get a better result with the correct stitches. (See also 'What drape/handle do you want?', on page 19.)

Knitting Basics

Holding the needles and yarn

Everyone has their own way of holding knitting needles. Some tuck one needle under their arm, some work with both needles over their wrists and some with the needles loose under their wrists. Once you have mastered the basic stitches you will probably have developed your own most comfortable holding position. If you do find your wrists, fingers or elbows aching, it may be that you are just getting used to holding the needles and are a bit tense because you are learning new techniques. If it persists, however, try holding your needles differently.

Making a slipknot

1 To make a slipknot, fold the working yarn in front of the tail end to form a circle (Fig 9.1).

2 Pass the working yarn through the circle from back to front, to form a loop (Fig 9.2).

3 Slide the slipknot onto the left-hand needle. This forms the first stitch of the cast on stitches.

Casting on

1 Begin by holding the needle with the slipknot on it in your left hand. Draw up the slipknot so it is snug but not too tight. The empty needle is held in your right hand and the yarn is held and manipulated using your right hand.

2 Using the empty needle in your right hand, insert the right-hand needle into the front of the slipknot from front to back.

3 Using your right hand, take the yarn round the back of the right-hand needle, bring it to the front across the right-hand needle and hold to the right (Fig 9.3).

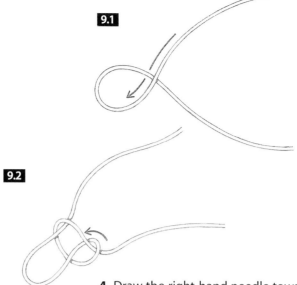

4 Draw the right-hand needle towards you, drawing a loop of yarn through the slipknot. You should have a loop of yarn on both needles.

5 To transfer the loop of yarn on the right-hand needle onto the left, twist the left-hand needle forwards and insert it into the front of the right-hand loop from front to back, right to left. You may need to draw the loop out a bit until you get used to this manoeuvre. If so, gently tighten up each stitch as you go so that it is snug, but not tight, on the needle (Fig 9.4).

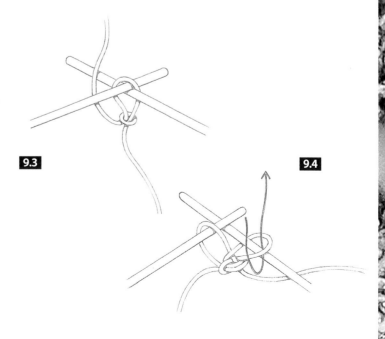

6 Remove the right-hand needle. You should now have two cast on stitches on the left hand needle.

7 Repeat this process, inserting the right-hand needle from front to back of the last stitch worked until you have cast on the number of stitches specified in your pattern (Fig 9.5).

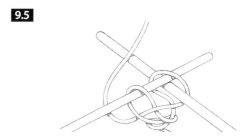

Garter stitch, knit stitch, or plain knitting

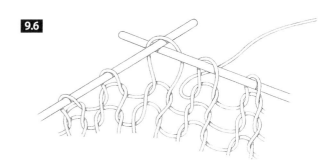

Garter stitch (also referred to as knit stitch or in some patterns as 'plain' knitting), is the first stitch most people learn. Garter stitch is reversible and is characterized by its alternate rows of ridges and bumps.

If you've mastered casting on you've done most of the stitch already, the main difference being that once you start knitting as opposed to casting on, your stitches will move from the left-hand needle to the right.

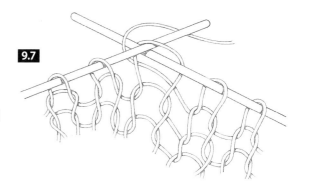

1 Hold the needle with the worked (or cast on) stitches in your left hand. The right hand holds the needle onto which the worked stitches will be transferred and holds the yarn at the back of the work.

2 Insert the right-hand needle from front to back into the front of the stitch nearest the point of the left needle (Fig 9.6). Bring the yarn towards you from the back of the work, round the empty right-hand needle and hold to the right at the back of the work (Fig 9.7).

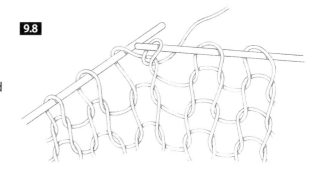

3 Bring the right-hand needle towards you, drawing a loop of yarn through the left-hand stitch (Fig 9.8).

4 Gently slip the left-hand needle out of the new stitch, keeping the new stitch on the right-hand needle (Fig 9.9).

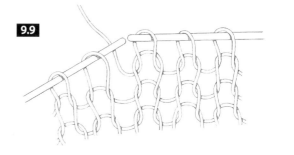

5 This forms your first garter stitch (referred to in most patterns as knit and abbreviated to K).

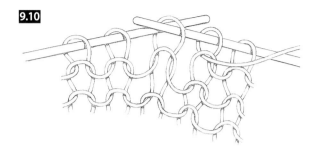

9.10

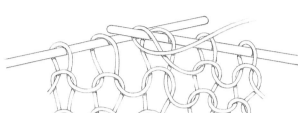

9.11

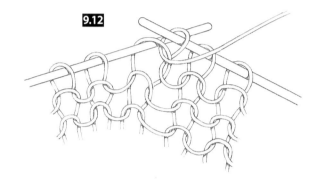

9.12

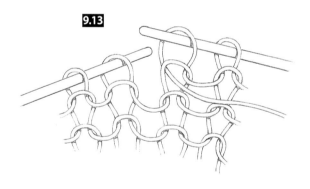

9.13

6 Continue in this way until all the cast on stitches have been worked.

7 Once you have worked all the stitches on the left-hand needle, swap your needles into the other hand. You should now have all the stitches and the first worked row on the left-hand needle, and an empty needle in your right hand again. The yarn is attached to the last stitch (nearest the needle point), on the left needle. (When you are learning, it is a good idea to count your stitches at this point to make sure you haven't gained or lost any.)

8 Keeping the empty needle in the right hand, pick up the yarn and hold in the right hand at the back of the work as before.

9 Work a garter (K) stitch into each stitch on the left needle as above.

Purl knitting
(purling or purl stitch)

1 Hold the needle with the worked (or cast on) stitches in your left hand. The right hand holds the needle onto which the worked stitches will be transferred and holds the yarn at the front of the work.

2 Insert the right-hand needle from the back to the front of the stitch nearest the point of the needle (Fig 9.10).

3 Take the yarn away from you towards the back of the work, round the empty right-hand needle, bring forward and hold to the right at the front of the work (Fig 9.11).

4 Take the right-hand needle away from you, drawing a loop of yarn through the left-hand stitch towards the back of the work (Fig 9.12).

5 Gently slip the left-hand needle out of the new stitch, keeping the new stitch on the right-hand needle and the yarn at the front (Fig 9.13).

6 This forms your first purl stitch, which is normally abbreviated in patterns to, simply, P.

7 Continue in this way until all the stitches have been worked.

8 Once you have worked all the stitches on the left-hand needle, swap your needles into the other hand. You should now have all the stitches and the first worked row on the left-hand needle, and an empty needle in your right hand again. The yarn is attached to the last stitch (nearest the needle point), on the left needle. (When you are first learning, it is a good idea to count your stitches at this point to make sure you haven't gained or lost any.)

9 Keeping the empty needle in the right hand, pick up the yarn and hold in the right hand at the front of the work as before.

10 Work a purl stitch into each stitch on the left needle as above.

Stocking stitch (stockinette stitch)

Stocking or stockinette stitch simply describes a fabric that is made from one row of garter (knit) stitch alternated with one row of purl stitch. The fabric is characterized by a very smooth side with 'V' shaped interlocking stitches and a more solid, bumpy side. With the smooth side facing you, this is normally regarded as the right side and a knit row is to be worked to maintain the stocking stitch pattern.

With the wrong (bumpy) side facing, a purl row is worked to preserve the stocking stitch effect. Stocking stitch is abbreviated in patterns to st st.

Casting off (binding off)

Casting or binding off is essentially a way of removing blocks of stitches in one go. Casting off fulfils two essential purposes: ending a piece of work by removing all of the stitches on the needle at once, and removing a number of stitches in one go to achieve certain shaping effects.

Casting off on either a knit or purl row follows, essentially, the same principles:

1 In each case two stitches are worked in the normal way and transferred onto the right-hand needle (either in a knit or purl stitch depending on the pattern). The first stitch is lifted over the second and dropped, leaving only the second stitch on the right-hand needle (Figs 9.14 and 9.15).

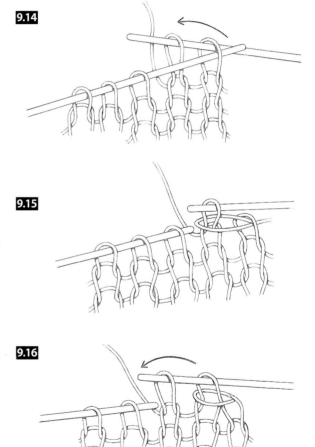

9.14

9.15

9.16

2 A third stitch is worked. The second stitch is then lifted over this stitch and dropped, leaving only the third stitch on the needle (Fig 9.16).

3 This process is repeated until all (or the specified number) of stitches have been cast off (Fig 9.17). In patterns, where a set number of cast off stitches are required, this refers only to the number of stitches lifted and dropped off. The stitch remaining on the right-hand needle does not count as one of the cast off stitches.

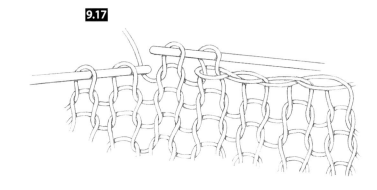

9.17

Decreasing

A less radical form of shaping and reducing stitch numbers is achieved by decreasing. This can be done in a number of ways and can be either functional, decorative (for certain pattern stitches), or both. For our purposes, we will only be using one decreasing method, working two stitches together. As with casting off, working two stitches together is essentially the same whether using garter stitch or purl.

Decrease 'knit-wise' (K2 tog)

1 To decrease (commonly abbreviated to 'dec') one stitch 'knit-wise', i.e. on a knit row, work a normal knit stitch, but instead of putting the right-hand needle into just the next stitch on the left-hand needle, insert the needle into the front of the next two stitches working from front to back (Fig 9.18).

2 Bring the yarn towards you from the back of the work, round the empty needle and hold to the right at the back of the work.

3 Bring the right-hand needle towards you, drawing a loop of yarn through both of the left-hand stitches.

4 Gently slip the left-hand needle out of the new stitch, keeping the new stitch on the right-hand needle.

5 This forms your first decrease stitch, referred to in patterns as knit two together or K2tog.

Decrease 'purl-wise' (P2tog)

1 A 'purl-wise' decrease ('dec'), on the other hand, occurs on a purl row, but is otherwise the same principle, i.e. on a purl row, work a normal purl stitch, but instead of putting the right-hand needle into just the next stitch on the left-hand needle, insert the needle into the front of the next two stitches working from back to front (Fig 9.19).

9.18

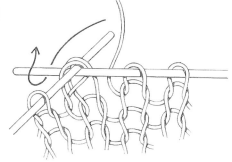

9.19

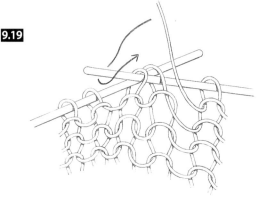

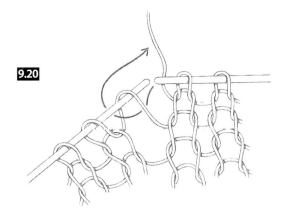

9.20

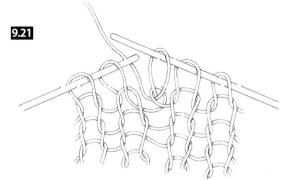

9.21

2 Bring the yarn away from you towards the back of the work, round the empty needle and hold to the right at the front of the work.

3 Bring the right-hand needle away from you, drawing a loop of yarn through both of the left-hand stitches.

4 Gently slip the left-hand needle out of the new stitch, keeping the new stitch on the right-hand needle.

5 This forms your first decrease stitch, referred to in patterns as purl two together or P2tog.

Increasing

Increasing stitches is also a means of shaping. Abbreviated either to inc or M1 (make one) in patterns, increasing stitches can be done in various ways, for purely practical purposes, for decorative effects, or for a combination of both.

Again, I have limited myself to describing one of the most common forms of increasing and one which will work for all the patterns in this book. I have used what is referred to as a 'lifted' increase, so-called because the new stitch is 'lifted' from between the two stitches below it and then knitted to form the new stitch.

Increase or make one 'knit-wise' ('M1')
As the name suggests increase or make one knit-wise usually occurs on a knit row.

1 To increase one stitch knit-wise, using the left-hand needle, pick up the thread which is between the stitches on the left- and

right-hand needles picking up from front to back and leaving the thread which will form the new stitch on the left-hand needle.

2 With the right-hand needle, knit the new stitch into the back of the loop, working from front to back (Fig 9.20).

3 Ease the new stitch onto the right-hand needle.

4 Knit the next stitch in the normal way (Fig 9.21).

5 One stitch has been increased.

Increase or make one 'purl-wise' ('M1')
Purl-wise increases occur on purl rows and are worked as follows:

1 Lift the loop between the stitches on the two needles as for a knit-wise increase above and keeping the new loop on the left-hand needle.

2 With the yarn to the front as normal, work a purl stitch but work the stitch through the back of the loop as shown in Fig 9.22.

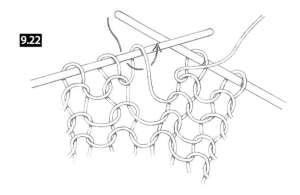

9.22

3 Ease the new stitch onto the right-hand needle.

4 Purl the next stitch as normal (Fig 9.23).

5 One purl-wise increase completed.

Joining in a new ball of yarn

There are a number of views as to the mechanics of joining in a new ball of yarn.

9.23

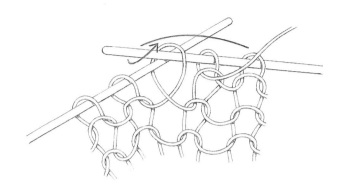

Row end

The simplest is to reach the end of a row, put a temporary knot in the two yarns at the start of the next row, and start knitting with the new yarn. When making up, the knot is undone and the yarn ends are woven in and trimmed accordingly.

I find that, whilst this approach works fine for seam edges, it is not a neat edge for a neckline or front edge, particularly when working with a fine yarn. This is, however, my preferred join for stripes where it is necessary always to begin a row with the new colour if a complete stripe of the new yarn is to be made.

Overlapping method

Another approach, which can be used in the middle of a row, is to overlap the two yarns, working with both yarns for a number of stitches, then dropping the 'old' yarn and continuing to work in the new. Again, when making up, any loose ends are darned in and trimmed.

This method has the advantage of being able to be worked anywhere in a row, but again, I find that it can cause a bulky patch where the two yarns are worked. This is not a particular issue with fluffy or slubby yarns (unless the slubs come together in the same place). However, with a very smooth pattern or a very fine yarn, the join can be seen and can spoil the overall look.

Temporary knot method

My preferred method (other than for stripes) is to place a temporary knot in the two yarns and continue knitting as normal. Aim to keep the knot to the wrong side of the work and adjust its positioning as required to achieve this. Leave 4in (10cm) of both the old and new yarn below the knot as this will be needed for stitching in later.

When making up, carefully undo the knot. Then, place a single knot in the two yarns. Draw up the single knot very gently until it is more or less flat with the knitted fabric. Weave in the two loose ends, working in opposite directions to the direction of the yarn in the knitting. So, as you are working on the wrong side of the fabric, the new yarn should be woven into the right and the old to the left. Weave the ends back on themselves for a couple of stitches then snip close to the fabric.

With this technique the temporary knot holds the two yarns together, but doesn't allow the stitch where the yarns join to stretch or spread. When the knot is undone, placing a single knot in the yarn holds the stitches either side in place, but without causing any puckering or holes. Because the yarns are woven in opposite directions, this also keeps the stitches firm but not pulled. Weaving in the ends rather than knitting with two yarns reduces bulk at the join. Joins can also be made anywhere in the row.

Crochet Basics

As the majority of readers will be right-handed, these instructions are written from that perspective. If you are left-handed, simply reverse the instructions. I have described the most commonly used method of holding the yarn and hook. Different countries and cultures may use alternative techniques so, if you feel more comfortable using a different method, that's fine. As long as your technique allows you to produce a consistent tension, work with whatever technique is most natural to you.

Making a slipknot

1 To make a slipknot, fold the working yarn in front of the tail end to form a circle (see Fig 9.1 on page 111).

2 Pass the working yarn through the circle from back to front, to form a loop (see Fig. 9.2 on page 111).

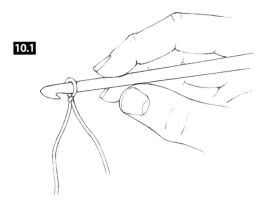

10.1

3 With the crochet hook held like a pencil in the right hand, use the middle finger to support the hook underneath (Fig 10.1). Place the hook through the loop and gently draw the loop tighter. The loop should not be too tight on the hook, or it will be difficult to draw it off the hook when making the stitches.

Holding the yarn

4 Still holding the hook in your right hand, wrap the main yarn around the fingers of your left hand (Fig 10.2). Again, hold the yarn firmly but not tightly, so as to ensure an even tension and a smooth, comfortable stitching position.

5 Keeping the main yarn in place around the fingers, take hold of the slipknot with the first and second fingers of your left hand. Raise the middle finger, holding it back slightly to allow it to work the yarn.

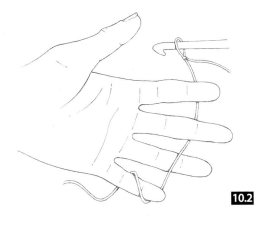

10.2

Making a chain

6 Wrap the main yarn around the hook, taking the yarn behind the hook, bringing it forwards and then taking it back under the hook. Hold the yarn back firmly (but not tightly) with your middle finger, to ensure that it remains under the hook (Fig 10.3).

10.3

7 Draw the hook back through the loop, thus forming a chain stitch.

8 Repeat steps 6 and 7 until you have made as many chain stitches as you need (Fig 10.4).

Crochet stitches

There are a considerable number of crochet stitches, many of which are variants on a basic theme. Illustrated below are three of the most commonly used stitches, slip stitch, double crochet and treble crochet. Explanation of a number of other stitches is also provided, although not illustrated.

Making a basic crocheted fabric

Please note that pattern instructions use US terminology, see headings and Appendix G (page 151) for UK equivalents.

A crocheted fabric generally uses as its base a number of chain stitches. These stitches are then worked upon either in rows (a 'straight' fabric) or by joining up the chain into a circle (working 'in the round').

Straight fabric – single crochet stitch ('sc' or UK double crochet 'dc')

1 For a straight fabric using a single crochet ('sc') stitch, make a number of chain ('ch') stitches. Insert the hook from front to back into the second chain from the hook. Ensure that the hook goes into the bottom of the chain, creating two threads on the hook in addition to the original chain (Fig 10.5).

2 Wrap the main yarn round the hook ('yrh'), bringing it from the back of the work, over the front of the hook, under the hook and to the back (Fig 10.6).

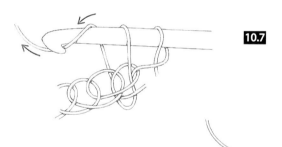

3 Draw the hook back through the chain, leaving the original loop, plus a new loop on the hook (Fig 10.7).

4 Yrh again and draw back through the two loops on the hook, leaving a single loop (Fig 10.8).

5 Insert the hook into the bottom of the next chain and repeat steps 2, 3, and 4 to make the next stitch.

6 Continue to repeat steps 2, 3 and 4 until a stitch has been made in each chain.

7 Make one chain stitch (Fig 10.9). This stitch is known as the turning chain ('tc') (see page 123).

8 Next, turn the work over from right to left so that the row of stitches you have just completed is now on the left of the hook (Fig 10.10).

9 Miss the first stitch of the previous row and work a single crochet into the second stitch (Fig 10.11). The hook should normally be inserted under the two horizontal loops at the top of the work. Different effects can be created, however, by inserting the hook into just the back loop or just the front loop. Your pattern will tell you when this is the case.

10 Continue making a single crochet into each stitch of the previous row until you reach the end of the row.

11 At the end of the row make a final single crochet into the turning chain of the previous row (Fig 10.12). This can be a little awkward, but a stitch worked into the turning chain will give a neater edge than working the stitch into the space between the chain and the last stitch.

Straight fabric – double crochet stitch ('dc', UK treble crochet stitch 'tr')

1 For a double crochet ('dc') fabric, make a number of chain stitches. Wrap the yarn around the hook ('yrh') (Fig 10.13). Next, insert the hook into the fourth chain from the hook, ensuring that the hook goes into the bottom of the chain.

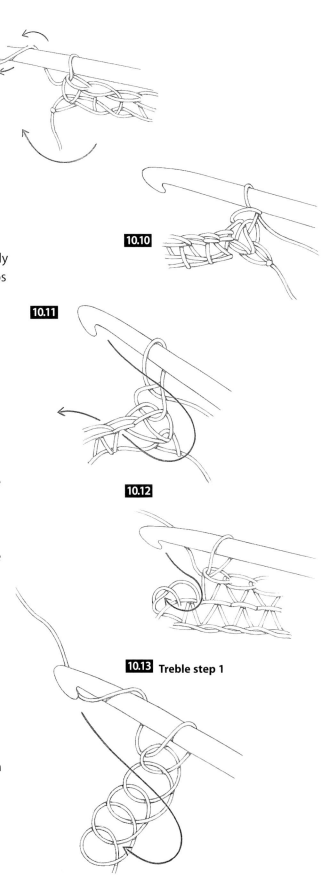

10.9

10.10

10.11

10.12

10.13 Treble step 1

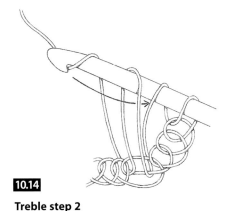

10.14
Treble step 2

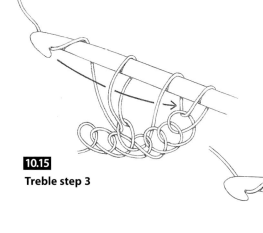

10.15
Treble step 3

10.16
Treble step 4

2 Yrh and draw the hook back through the chain (Fig 10.14). You should now have three loops (lps) in total on the hook (Fig 10.15).

3 Yrh, then draw the hook back under two lps, leaving two lps on the hook (Fig 10.16).

4 Yrh, then draw the hook back under two lps, leaving one lp on the hook and completing the double crochet stitch (Fig 10.17).

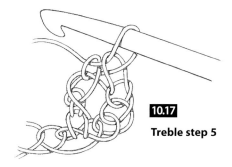

10.17
Treble step 5

5 Yrh and insert the hook from front to back into the next chain.

6 Repeat steps 2, 3, 4 and 5 to continue making a double crochet into each stitch of the previous row until you reach the end of the row.

7 At the end of the row make a final double crochet into the last stitch of the turning chain of the previous row. This can be a little awkward, but a stitch worked into the turning chain will give a neater edge than working the stitch into the space between the chain and the last stitch.

8 Make three chain stitches. These stitches form the turning chain (see page 123).

9 Next, turn the work over from right to left so that the row of stitches you have just completed is now on the left of the hook.

10 Miss the first stitch of the previous row and work double crochet into the second stitch. The hook should normally be inserted below the two horizontal loops at the top of the work. However, as with single crochet, different effects can be created by inserting the hook into just the back loop, just the front loop or into the space between the stitches. This will be indicated by the pattern.

Straight fabric – half double crochet ('hdc', UK half treble 'htr')

1 For a half double crochet ('hdc') fabric, make a number of chain stitches. Wrap the yarn around the hook ('yrh') then insert the hook into the third chain from the hook, ensuring that the hook goes into the bottom of the chain.

2 Draw the hook back through the chain. You should now have three loops (lps) in total on the hook.

3 Yrh, draw back through all three lps, leaving one lp on the hook. This completes the first half double crochet.

4 Yrh and insert the hook into the bottom of the next chain.

5 Repeat steps 2, 3, and 4 to make the next stitch until a half double crochet stitch has been made in each chain.

6 Make two chain stitches. These stitches form the turning chain (see above).

7 Next, turn the work over from right to left so that the row of stitches you have just completed is now on the left of the hook.

8 Miss the first stitch of the previous row and work a half double crochet into the second stitch. The hook should normally be inserted below the two horizontal loops at the top of the work. However, as with single crochet, different effects can be created by inserting the hook into just the back loop, just the front loop or into the space between the stitches. This will be indicated by the pattern.

Slip stitch

As slip stitches have little height, they are rarely used as a 'pattern' stitch. They do, however, have a number of uses:

● to join the ends of a round when working on a circular piece
● to form a cord (useful for drawstrings/straps)
● for shaping and moving between different areas of a fabric
● when making buttonholes.

1 To make a slip stitch, first make a chain then insert the hook from front to back into the second stitch in the chain.

2 Wrap the yarn round the hook and draw the yarn through all the loops on the hook, leaving only the working loop. This forms a slip stitch.

3 Further slip stitches can be made by repeating this process. No turning chain are required when working with slip stitches as the stitch has no height.

Turning chain

The purpose of the turning chain is to allow for the height of the stitch. The turning chain counts as the first stitch of the new row and the number of stitches worked for the turning chain will vary depending on the height of the stitch being worked (see the table on page 128). The first stitch in the row is then missed to allow for the turning chain.

Increasing gradually

Gradual increases to form a curve can be achieved quite easily by simply working twice into one stitch (Fig 10.18). Your pattern instructions should tell you where to make your increases depending on the effect to be achieved.

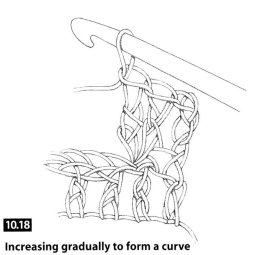

10.18
Increasing gradually to form a curve

Increasing a number of stitches at once

It is possible to increase several stitches at once, however, different techniques are used depending on whether the increases are to be made at the beginning or end of the row.

Increases at the beginning of a row

1 For increases at the beginning of a row work the normal number of turning chain plus the number of extra stitches you need (Fig 10.19). For example, if you need to increase by 6 stitches in single crochet, make 7 chain, being 1 turning chain and 6 extra stitches; for 6 double crochet stitches, make 9 chain, being 3 turning chain and 6 extra stitches.

2 Work the first single crochet into the second chain from the hook.

3 Work a single crochet into each extra chain.

4 Continue to work in single crochet until the end of the row as normal.

5 At the end of the next row, simply work across the extra stitches as normal, working the turning chain at the end in the usual way.

Increases at the end of a row

1 To increase stitches at the end of a row, work across the row until two stitches remain, including the stitch normally worked into the turning chain (Fig 10.20).

2 Leave the working loop on a spare hook/stitch holder or pin.

3 Take a spare length of the yarn you are using and make a length of chain equal to the number of extra stitches you need.

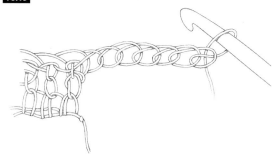

10.19

Increasing several stitches at once at the start of a row

4 Join this chain to the end of the row with a slip stitch and fasten off.

5 Put the working loop back on the correct hook and work one stitch into each of the last two stitches.

6 Work a single crochet (or the stitch being used) into each of the new chain you have just joined on.

7 Turn the work from right to left, make a turning chain and work across all the stitches including the new stitches you have added.

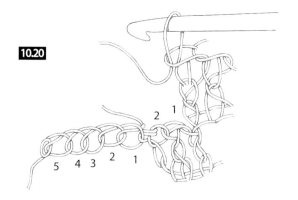

10.20

Increasing several stitches at once at the end of a row

Decreasing gradually

To make a gradual decrease you could simply miss a stitch. However, unless this is specifically intended to be part of the pattern, this method may leave an unsightly hole. As an alternative, gradual decreases may be made in the following way:

At the beginning of a row:
1 Make the appropriate number of turning chain and miss the first stitch as normal.

2 Work your stitch in the usual way until 2 lps remain on the hook.

3 Keeping the 2 lps on the hook, yrh if required (for example, if working in double crochet/half double crochet, and so on) and then insert the hook into the next stitch.

4 Follow the normal steps in making the stitch until there are 3 lps on the hook in total.

5 Yrh and draw through all 3 lps (1 lp remaining).

6 Continue to the end of the row.

For example, to decrease one double crochet:
1 After working the turning chain, yrh then insert hook into second stitch.

2 Yrh and draw hook through chain.

3 Yrh and draw through 2 lps (2 lps remain).

4 Yrh and insert hook into next stitch.

5 Yrh and draw hook through chain (4 lps on hook).

6 Yrh and draw through 2 lps (3 lps remaining).

7 Yrh and draw through all 3 lps to complete the decrease (1 lp remaining).

At the end of a row:

For stitch decreases at the end of a row the process is the same, but bear in mind that it is neater to make any decrease before the very end of the row. For this reason, to decrease at the end of a row work to the last 3 stitches, including the turning chain from the previous row.

For example, to decrease one double crochet:
1 Work to the last 3 stitches of the row including the turning chain.

2 Yrh then insert hook into next stitch.

3 Yrh and draw hook through chain.

4 Yrh and draw through 2 lps (2 lps remain).

5 Yrh and insert hook into next stitch.

6 Yrh and draw hook through chain (4 lps on hook).

7 Yrh and draw through 2 lps (3 lps remaining).

8 Yrh and draw through all 3 lps to complete the decrease (1 lp remaining).

9 Work the turning chain of the previous row to complete the row.

Decreasing a number of stitches at once

At the beginning of a row
1 Work a slip stitch into each stitch until the correct number of stitches to be decreased has been reached.

2 Work one more slip stitch then work the correct number of turning chain for the stitch being used.

3 Complete the row as normal, checking that the correct number of stitches have been decreased.

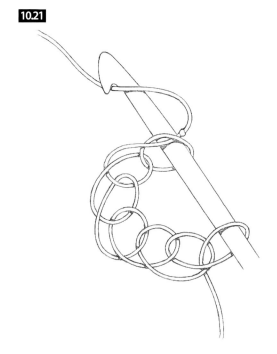

Note

Common Mistakes
If your work is narrowing with each row and the number of stitches is decreasing, the likelihood is that either:

● *you have not worked a stitch into the turning chain at the end of each row, or*
● *a stitch has been missed somewhere along the row.*

Conversely, if your work is getting wider, and the number of stitches in the row is increasing, it is likely that either:

● *the first stitch of the row has been worked instead of being missed, or*
● *a stitch along the row has been worked into twice.*

At the end of a row

1 Work the row as normal simply leaving the number of stitches to be decreased unworked. (Remember to count the turning chain from the previous row as one of the stitches.)

2 Make the correct number of turning chain for the stitch being used, turn and continue as normal.

Working in the round

Working crochet 'in the round' is, in many respects, more flexible than knitting if you intend to make tubular shapes for bolster cushions, hats, or any other item which requires a circle as part of its shape. Hats in particular are ideally suited to this technique.

The stitches used for crocheting in the round are the same as those used to make a 'straight' fabric. The key difference with working in the round is that the work is never turned over (see step 8 in the single crochet

section, page 121). Rather, at the end of each round, the work is continued by slip stitching the first to the last stitch.

As with straight fabrics it is still necessary to work a number of chain at the end of each round, and we use the same number as for an ordinary turning chain, depending on the stitch being used (so one for a single crochet, three for a double crochet, and so on).

Each pattern will differ, depending on the style and design requirements, but try this example to give you an idea of the principles and techniques involved:

1 For a circle using double crochet stitch, begin with 6 chain.

2 Join up the circle by making a slip stitch into the first chain worked (Fig 10.21).

3 Next, make 3 chain. These will form the first stitch and are the equivalent of the turning chain in a flat, straight fabric.

10.21

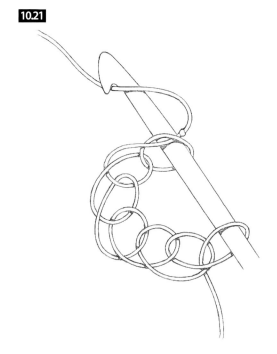

Working a circle, step 1

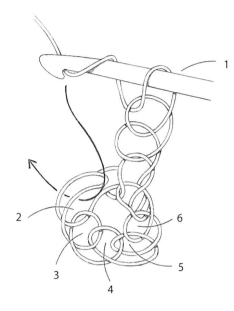

4 Work a double crochet into each chain stitch (Fig 10.22).

5 When you have completed your 6 double crochet (5 dc plus dc made by the turning chain), join the last double crochet worked to the top of the chain stitch you made at step 3 above. You should now have 6 double crochet stitches in the circle, including the 3 chain worked at step 3 above.

6 Make 3 chain.

7 Work 2 double crochet into each stitch around the circle (10dc in total, plus the turning chain to make 11).

8 To complete the round, work a double crochet into the base of the first 3 chain.

9 Using a slip stitch join this double crochet to the top of the chain as before. You should now have increased your stitches to 12.

10 Make 3 chain.

11 For the third round work 1 double crochet into the next stitch and 2 double crochet stitches into the next.

12 Continue in this way, working two double crochet stitches into every other stitch.

13 At the end of the round, work your final double crochet into the base of the chain on the previous round.

14 Slip stitch the final double crochet to the top stitch of the chain at the beginning of the round as before. You should now have 18 stitches.

15 For the next round make your three chain as before and work a double crochet into every third stitch (so 1dc, 1dc, 2dc, 1dc, 1dc, 2dc and so on).

16 Make the final double crochet into the base of the chain on the previous row and slip stitch the final double crochet to the top chain at the start of the round as before (24 stitches).

You should by now be able to see how your stitching is producing a flat circle. Depending on the stitch used and the yarn, you may find that your pattern increases at a different rate or starts with more or fewer stitches. When making a hat, for example, you don't necessarily want a flat circle, so the pattern of increases will be designed to give a curve to accommodate the shape of the head. These should all be made clear, however, in the pattern instructions and providing you follow the instructions you should achieve the desired results.

Turning Chain for Each Type of Stitch

US	UK	Turning chain
Slip stitch (sl st)	Slip stitch	0
Single crochet (sc)	Double crochet (dc)	1
Half double crochet (hdc)	Half treble (htr)	2
Double crochet (dc)	Treble (tr)	3
Treble (tr)	Double treble (dtr)	4

Finishing Touches

Making Up

There are many types of seams and stitches for joining knitted and crochet fabrics. The following instructions are for the three simplest and most commonly used joining methods, which can be used in a wide variety of circumstances without looking unsightly. If you would like to explore other methods, there are many good knitting and crochet technique books which can take you on to the next stage.

Overcasting

This simple seaming technique does not produce a seam as firm as backstitch (see below), but is flatter and less bulky for areas which won't be under a lot of stretching and strain.

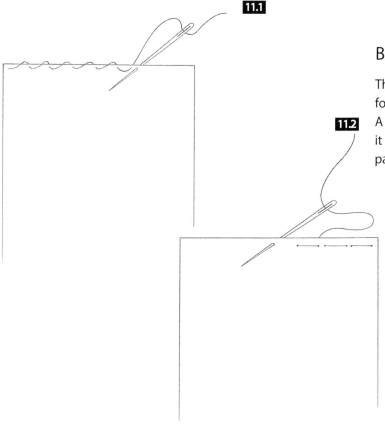

1 Place the two edges to be overcast together; normally this means the right sides are placed facing each other but, if this is not appropriate for the pattern (e.g. for a decorative stitch), this will be made clear in the instructions.

2 Secure the yarn at the start of the seam by sewing two small stitches on top of one another through both layers of the fabric. If you are right-handed, work from left to right. Left-handers may prefer to work right to left.

3 Overcast as shown in Fig 11.1 working the stitches firmly but not so tightly as to pucker the work.

4 At the end of the seam, make a couple of tiny stitches, thread the yarn carefully back through the seam and fasten off.

Backstitch

This is probably the most familiar stitch for knitting, crochet and sewing seams. A good all-rounder, strong and simple, but it can be a little bulky in some circumstances, particularly on babywear and very fine work.

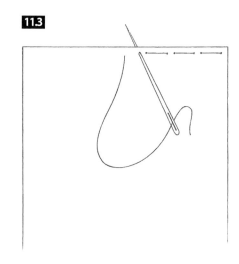

1 First place the two pieces with right sides together. Secure the yarn (right-hand end for right-handers, left for left-handers) with two small stitches on top of one another.

2 With the yarn at the back of the work, bring the needle up a short distance to the left of the first two securing stitches from back to front of the work.

3 Re-insert the needle from front to back of the work, at the end of the previous stitch (for the first stitch, this will be where the two securing stitches were made).

4 Bring the needle up again from front to back, again slightly to the left of the last stitch, (see Fig 11.2, facing page), $^1/_{16}$–$^1/_8$in (2–3mm), depending on the thickness of the fabric.

5 Take the yarn back down through the fabric at the end of the last stitch (see Fig 11.3, facing page).

6 When the seam has been completed, make a couple of tiny stitches on top of one another, thread the yarn carefully back through the seam a little way and fasten off.

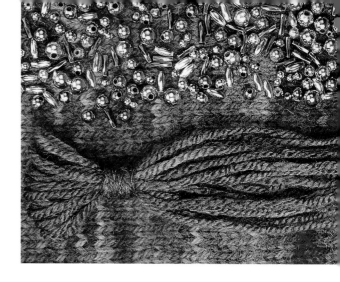

Embellishments

Tassels

Tassels are quick and easy to make. Used on clothes, accessories or soft furnishings they can be fun and funky, or smart and stylish, depending on the yarns used. Metallic yarns, ribbon or beads can be added and the size and length varied to suit the piece.

I describe a very simple technique here, but there are a number of tassel-making gadgets on the market which allow you to be more creative, if you prefer.

Method

1 Cut approx. 12 pieces of yarn, each 12in (30cm) long. Fold in half and use a further piece of yarn to wrap around the folded, halved strands starting wrapping at about ³⁄₄in (1.5cm) from the folded end, and continuing for ³⁄₄in (1.5cm). Make your wrapping quite tight and finish off as neatly as possible by running the thread back up through the wrapping then back down again (Fig 11.4).

2 To attach the tassel, pass a new piece of thread several times through the loop formed by the folded yarns, then through the item, until the tassel feels firmly attached; don't pull the thread too tight, as the tassel must have some movement (Fig 11.5).

3 Trim the ends of the tassel to broadly equal lengths.

11.4

11.5

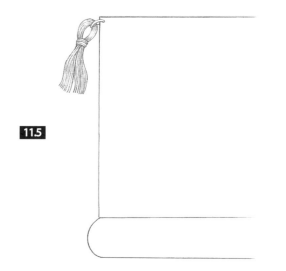

Direction of weaving

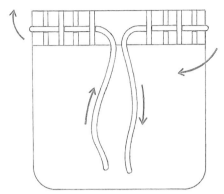

Simple drawstring

1 Measure around the circumference of the opening.

2 Make a drawstring from a crocheted chain, length of ribbon, twisted cord or similar. The drawstring should be double the circumference of the opening, to allow the bag to be opened fully without the drawstring ends disappearing into the bag.

3 Starting where the drawstring is to be drawn up (usually the front or side), weave the drawstring in and out of the holes (Fig. 11.6).

4 The ends of your drawstring should meet, and can be drawn up as required. At this stage, any tassels/beads or other embellishments may be added at the ends of the drawstring.

Double drawstring

Unlike the simple drawstring, the double drawstring is usually drawn up at either side and stitched or joined at the ends to form a single thread. Thus, the drawstring, when fully drawn up, can be used to slip over the wrist or hang an item up without any further additions.

1 Measure around the circumference of the opening.

2 Make a drawstring as above, but four times the circumference of the opening, to allow for the drawstring to be drawn up. This may be shorter or longer, depending on the design of the piece.

3 Fold your drawstring in half and mark the halfway point with a pin, or tie a spare piece of cotton round the cord at that point. Take one end of the drawstring and, starting at the side of the piece, weave it in and out of the holes (Fig 11.7) until you come back to the side where you started.

11.7 Double drawstring step 1

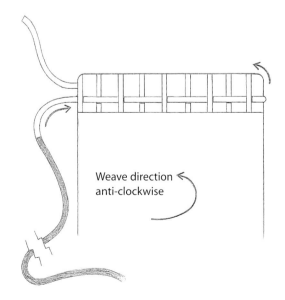

Weave direction anti-clockwise

4 Weave the other end of the cord in the opposite direction (Fig. 11.8), ensuring that the centre fold remains at the side of the piece at all times. Both ends should then finish at the same point, back where they started, with the halfway fold on the same side.

5 Loosely fasten the two ends together and loosen one of the loops on the opposite side of the piece. Draw this loop out until the loop with the joined ends and the new loop are broadly equal. Remove the pin/cotton at the halfway point.

6 Draw the two loops outwards to check that the drawstring works and adjust until the two loops are equal.

7 Unknot the temporarily joined ends and neatly fasten together with a couple of small stitches.

Adding beads

When you are looking for something to enhance a design, beads can be a good choice. Tiny seed beads or faux pearls look lovely on an evening bag (see projects 9 and 10), while chunky wooden or ceramic beads make ideal fasteners for a tote.

Try adding beads to a fringe or tassel, to give a little weight and a better drape. However, as with any embellishment, avoid 'overloading' your design and remember to choose beads of a suitable size for the fabric and purpose of the item.

11.8 **Double drawstring step 2**

a) End of ribbon woven anti-clockwise

b) End of ribbon woven clockwise

c) Halfway point in length of ribbon

Weave direction clockwise

step 1 weave
step 2 weave

When selecting beads, pay careful attention to the hole size. While it is possible to thread beads onto a yarn where the yarn is thicker than the hole in the bead, thought should be given to the look of the bead in the context of the yarn. Remember that a very fine bead with a very small hole, will – even if it can be threaded onto the yarn – be difficult to move along the yarn. Indeed, the friction caused by sliding the bead up and down may cause the yarn to fray, or even break.

Note

If you break a bead, or need to adjust the number used, break off the yarn, adjust the bead threading and rejoin the yarn in the normal way. Obviously you can't do this too often, but it can be done if necessary. For advice on buying beads, see page 94.

Tip

Method

When beads are added to a piece, they are all threaded onto the yarn before it is knitted/ crocheted so, where different beads are used, they must be threaded in the correct order.

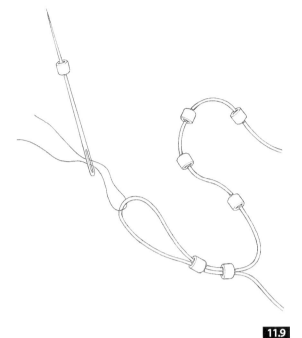

1 Thread the beads onto the yarn using a normal sewing needle, threaded with a standard cotton sewing thread. Loop the sewing thread over the yarn, then thread through the sewing needle, leaving a length of thread between the needle and the yarn (Fig 11.9).

2 Threading the beads in the correct order (if relevant), pass each bead onto the needle, over the fine sewing thread and over the loop onto the yarn.

11.9

3 Repeat this process for each bead.

Care of Hand-dyed Pieces

Fibre-reactive dyes are relatively robust and wash fast. However, you have put a lot of time and love into your project, so I recommend careful hand-washing to be on the safe side.

- A gentle, vegetable-based product, suitable for hand-washing woollens and silks is best – I use soap flakes, or a hand-wash liquid. Avoid biological detergents and anything containing optical brighteners or bleach, as these may fade the colours and damage the yarns.

- Do not soak the item, but rinse thoroughly.

- Avoid wringing; gently squeeze the item, then roll it carefully in a towel to soak up the excess moisture.

- If your item is bulky or gets lots of use (a rug, bag or blanket, for example), you may be able to wash in the machine using a wool cycle/program; put the item in an old pillow or duvet case, to reduce pilling and fluffing. Remember that the colour may come out into the washing water, so don't put anything else in the load which might be affected by stray colours in the wash.

- After washing, gently pull the item into shape and dry flat, if possible, either outside if the weather is fine, or in a warm airing cupboard or room, but not on a radiator or near direct heat. Some yarns can be gently tumble dried, but check the washing instructions first.

- If an item needs pressing, use a damp towel or cloth and apply a gentle pressing motion. Don't slide the iron, but lift and press to avoid any stretching. Be particularly careful with textured yarns, as the texture can be flattened by pressing.

Kits, Equipment and Yarn Stockists

United Kingdom

Yarns

The yarns used in the projects were all obtained from two suppliers (see below). Both suppliers sell by mail order and supply customers both in the UK and around the world. I have also provided details of a number of suppliers outside the UK who should be able to supply yarns of a similar type to those used, as well as a selection of websites with links to a wide range of suppliers.

William Hall & Co.
177 Stanley Road
Cheadle Hulme
Cheadle, Cheshire
SK8 6RF

Tel: + 44 (0) 161 437 3295
Email: william@hallyarns.fsnet.co.uk

Texere Yarns
College Mill
Barkerend Road
Bradford
BD1 4AU

Tel: + 44 (0) 1274 722191
Website: www.texereyarns.co.uk

Dyes

The dyes for the projects may be obtained from a variety of sources and I have listed a small number of these below. I used procion mx dyes from Fibrecrafts, but other suppliers sell similar dyes.

Kemtex Colours
Chorley Business & Technology Centre
Euxton Lane
Chorley, Lancashire
PR7 6TE

Tel: + 44 (0) 1257 230220
Website: www.kemtex.co.uk or www.textiledyes.co.uk

Fibrecrafts & George Weil
Old Portsmouth Road
Peasmarsh
Guildford
GU3 1LZ

Tel: + 44 (0) 1483 565800
Website: www.fibrecrafts.com

Equipment

Most of the equipment used in hand dyeing can be found in your local hardware or kitchenware store. Yard sales and thrift/secondhand shops are also a useful source of inexpensive pots, dishes and pans.

Needles, crochet hooks and similar items should be readily available from your local haberdashery/craft store.

Kits

As an alternative, I can supply kits for each of the projects. Kits are either yarn and dyes only (colours of your choice) or a full kit with both the yarns and dyes and the basic equipment required. Individual items may also be ordered. Please contact me via one of the routes listed below.

Debbie Tomkies
7 Fonthill Grove
Sale
Cheshire
M33 4FR

Tel: + 44 (0) 161 973 7390
Email: debbie.tomkies@dsl.pipex.com
Website: www.dtcrafts.com

Other useful addresses

Below I have listed details of a number of guilds, associations and useful websites. These are a great place to look for help with techniques, supplier lists, and practical information. Many have bulletin boards for tips and help and they can often put you in touch with groups, courses and events in your area. Perhaps more importantly, they are a great way to connect with fellow knitters and crafters wherever you may be in the world.

The Knitting and Crochet Guild
Central Coordinator
Margaret Howell
10 Marine Court
Fitzalan Road
Littlehampton
W Sussex
BN17 5NF

Tel: + 44 (0) 1903 732806
Website: www.knitting-and-crochetguild.org.uk

A members organization which, amongst many other things, runs exhibitions and demonstrations, arranges courses and sells knitting/crochet-related books, accessories and other goods.

The Guild has a number of regional contact groups which meet up on an ad hoc or more formalized basis. There is also a help service, a museum collection and a pattern library and the Guild has representatives in the UK, the US, Australia and New Zealand, with details on the above website or via the Central Coordinator (above).

The Association of Guilds of Weavers, Spinners and Dyers
Secretary
Ms P Bakker
3 Gatchell Meadow
Trull
Taunton
Somerset TA3 7HY

Tel: + 44 (0) 1823 325345
Website: www.wsd.org.uk

An organization with members and guilds worldwide. Publishes the Journal and arranges conferences, courses, exhibitions and similar events. Local guilds also arrange meetings, trips and other events, depending on members' interests. A focal point for craft enthusiasts with a particular interest in textiles.

United States of America

Earth Guild
33 Haywood Street
Asheville, NC 28801
USA

Tel: 1-800-327-8448
Website: www.earthguild.com

US-based supplier of yarns, dyes
and accessories – international
and web-based sales.

Patternworks
Route 25
Post Office Box 1618
Center Harbor, NH 03226–1618
USA

Tel (toll free): 800-4385464
Foreign: 603-253-8732
Email: customerservice@patternworks.com
Website: www.patternworks.com

Patternworks is a mail order catalogue that
has everything for the hand knitter.

NuMei
1320 Tall Maple Loop
Oviedo
Florida 32765
USA

Tel: 407-365-4724
Website: www.numei.com

US-based suppliers of yarn and accessories,
with international mail order and
web-based sales.

Canada

Handknitting.com
478 County Road 1, RR 8
Picton, Ontario K0K 2T0
Canada

Tel: 1-613-476-8913
Email: nanc@handknitting.com
Website: www.handknitting.com

This is an Internet-based retailer
located in Canada.

Knitting Guild of Canada
PO Box 444, 8 Victoria Street East
Princetown, Ontario N0J 1V0
Canada

Tel: (705) 722-6495
Website: www.cgknitters.ca

Australia

Australian Craft Network
Website: www.auscraftnet.com.au

Crochet Australia
Website: www.crochetaustralia.com.au
Email: vicki@crochetaustralia.com.au

The Wool Shack
Website: www.thewoolshack.com
Email: info@thewoolshack.com

Secure Internet knitting store, with all the
service and support of your local yarn store.

Appendix A: Yarn Record

SAMPLE NO.														
DATE:														
PROJECT REF (IF APPLICABLE):														
YARN DETAILS:														
YARN NAME	YARN TYPE (DK/ARAN etc.)	FIBRE CONTENT (e.g. 50:50 COTTON/ SILK, 100% WOOL)	SUPPLIER	PRICE										

SWATCH DETAILS

CROCHET/KNIT	NEEDLE/ HOOK SIZE	STITCHES USED	STITCHES IN 10cm	ROWS IN 10cm	TOTAL STITCHES IN SAMPLE	TOTAL ROWS IN SAMPLE	SIZE OF COMPLETE SWATCH (area in sq in/cm²)*	WEIGHT OF SWATCH

ADDITIONAL NOTES

Use this space to describe the feel of the yarn, its drape and texture. Make a note of any properties which would influence its suitability for a given project (e.g. too hairy/rough for a jumper, avoid using for garments that will be close to the skin)

* To calculate the area of the swatch, simply multiply the total length by the total width of the swatch after pressing. For example, a swatch 5½in (14cm) wide by 5in (13cm) in length will be 5½ x 5in (14 x 13cm) = 27½sq in (182cm²)

Appendix B: Dyeing Record

DYEING RECORD SHEET

DATE:

BATCH NO:

PROJECT REF (IF APPLICABLE):

YARN DETAILS:

NAME	TYPE (DK, sport, aran etc.)	YARN CONTENT	SUPPLIER	WEIGHT

PRE-SOAK DETAILS:

YARN WEIGHT	SALT	FIXER (VINEGAR) (PROTEIN FIBRES)	FIXER (SODIUM CARBONATE) (CELLULOSE FIBRES)	WATER

DYES:

DYE TYPE	BRAND	SUPPLIER	COLOUR	VOLUME of dye solution	CONCENTRATION (% strength)

METHOD USED:

1

2

3

4

5

6

7

Additional notes: (e.g. 1% dye too strong. Try 0.25% on next batch)

How to calculate the quantities of levelling agent, fixative and water required for a given project using the hot water method

Protein (animal) yarns

For protein yarns such as wool, angora, cashmere, alpaca (and silk if using the hot water method), use the following table to calculate the amount of levelling agent, fixative and water needed for the amount of yarn being dyed:

Amount of yarn
U.S./Imperial

Weight of yarn oz/lb	Levelling agent (salt) oz (tsp)	Fixative (vinegar) fl oz (cups)	Water cups (gal)
$\frac{1}{2}$oz	$\frac{1}{8}$oz ($\frac{3}{4}$tsp)	$\frac{1}{2}$fl oz	2 cups
1oz	$\frac{1}{4}$oz ($1\frac{1}{2}$tsp)	1fl oz	$3\frac{3}{4}$ cups
10oz	$2\frac{1}{2}$oz	10fl oz ($1\frac{1}{4}$ cups)	$37\frac{1}{2}$ cups ($2\frac{1}{4}$gal)
1lb	4oz	16fl oz (2 cups)	60 cups ($3\frac{3}{4}$gal)

Metric

Weight of yarn g/kg	Levelling agent (salt) g	Fixative (vinegar) ml (litre)	Water litres
10g	2.5g	10ml	0.3 (300ml)
50g	12.5g	50ml	1.5l
100g	25g	100ml	3l
500g	125g	500ml	15l
1,000g (1kg)	250g	1,000ml (1 litre)	30l

Note:

For mixtures of animal and plant fibres, more care will be required. Both types of fixative (vinegar and sodium carbonate) should be included in the soaking solution. The amounts of each should be calculated either by apportioning based on the fibre mix, or by using the same amount of each fixative as would normally be used if the fibre were entirely of animal/plant composition. So, if you are dyeing 4oz (120g) of a 60:40 cotton:wool yarn, you should either calculate the amount of sodium carbonate fixative required for $2\frac{2}{3}$oz (72g) cotton and the amount of vinegar fixative for $1\frac{1}{3}$oz (48g) wool (the apportionment method), or alternatively, you could use enough of each fixative as if there were 4oz (120g) of each fibre (the total method). For the salt, the same approach may be followed, just make sure that you consistently use either the apportionment method or a total method for both salt and fixer.

As animal fibre yarns will not set satisfactorily without heat, it will be necessary to use the hot water method. This should not prevent any plant-based element in the yarn from setting, but you will need to test the yarn to ensure that it can withstand the necessary heat without felting, pilling or shrinking. The easiest way is to test a small skein first. First, soak it in a pre-soak solution with the appropriate amounts of salt, sodium carbonate and vinegar as specified above. Next, heat the yarn gently to minimize the stress to the yarn. If, when the yarn has been heated, cooled, rinsed and dried it looks okay, then you should be able to proceed with confidence. In my experience, most plant-based yarns are quite robust and can be hot dyed with care if required.

Appendix D

How to calculate the quantities of levelling agent, fixative and water required for a given project using the cold water method

Cellulose (plant) yarns

For cellulose yarns such as cotton, ramie, hemp, viscose, linen (and silk if using the cold water method), use the following table to calculate the amount of levelling agent, fixative and water needed for the amount of yarn being dyed:

Amount of yarn
US/Imperial

Weight of yarn oz/lb	Levelling agent (salt) oz	Fixative (sodium carbonate) oz	Water cups (gal)
$\frac{1}{2}$oz	$\frac{1}{4}$oz	$\frac{1}{8}$oz	2 cups
1oz	$\frac{1}{2}$oz	$\frac{1}{4}$oz	$3\frac{3}{4}$ cups
10oz	5oz	$2\frac{1}{2}$oz	$37\frac{1}{2}$ cups ($2\frac{1}{4}$gal)
1lb	8oz	4oz	60 cups ($3\frac{3}{4}$gal)

Metric

Weight of yarn g/kg	Levelling agent (salt) g	Fixative (sodium carbonate) g	Water litres
10g	5g	2.5g	0.3 (300ml)
50g	25g	12.5g	1.5l
100g	50g	25g	3l
500g	250g	125g	15l
1,000g (1kg)	500g	250g	30l

Note:

For mixed plant and animal fibre yarns, please see the special instructions for fixing these yarns in Appendix C.

Appendix E

How to make up stock solutions of dye

Dyes are generally purchased as powders and need to be dissolved in water before they are applied to the yarn. The resulting solution is referred to as a 'stock' solution. The strength of a stock solution is usually described as a percentage. A 1% solution is normally regarded as the 'standard' strength, with 2% being much stronger, 0.5% weaker, and so on.

For a 1% solution, use ⅕tsp (1g) of dye powder for every 3½ fl oz (100ml) of water. For example, if you need 17½ fl oz (500ml) of dye solution at 1%, you will need 1tsp (5g) of dye powder.

A 2% solution, which will be much stronger and produce a more intense colour, will contain ⅖tsp (2g) of dye powder but is still dissolved in 3½ fl oz (100ml) of water. So, to produce 17½ fl oz (500ml) dye solution at 2% strength, 2tsp (10g) of dye powder will be required.

For other amounts, use the following calculation to work out the weight of dye needed:

Volume of water x % dye strength required, then divide the resulting number by 100

If you purchase your dyes already in solution, ask the supplier what percentage strength the solution is. Then, simply work out how much dye solution you need, measure out the right amount from your ready-made stock solution and your dye should be ready to use.

The potential disadvantage with ready-made dye solutions is that it is not possible to make the dye stronger. If you need a stronger dye, you could ask your supplier if they stock stronger solutions. Alternatively, you may need to purchase powders. Weaker dyes can be obtained, however, by diluting the purchased solution.

How much dye will I need?

As yarns take up dye at different rates, it can be difficult to predict the quantity of dye solution you will require. As a broad guide, I generally work on the basis that 3½ fl oz (100ml) of dye at 1% strength (i.e. ⅕tsp [1g] dye to 3½ fl oz [100ml] water) should comfortably dye ⅔oz (20g) of most protein yarns, silk, viscose, and Lurex/viscose tapes or ribbons, to a good strong colour. A cotton yarn may, however, require more dye as these yarns tend to absorb dye less readily.

So, once you know how much yarn you want to dye, you can calculate the approximate amount of dye solution required simply by multiplying the amount of yarn in ounces by 5¼ to give the total dye solution required in fluid ounces; while, if you are working in UK metric, you will need to multiply the weight of yarn in grams by 5, to give you the total volume of dye solution needed in millilitres. For example, 10oz yarn would require 52½ fl oz dye solution (10oz x 5¼), while 300g yarn would require 1,500ml dye solution (300g x 5).

Volume of dye solution required (assuming 3½ fl oz [100ml] dye at 1% strength will dye ⅔oz [20g] yarn)

US/Imperial

Weight of yarn oz (lb)	Dye solution required fl oz (cups)
1oz	5¼ fl oz
10oz	52½ fl oz (6¼ cups)
1lb	84 fl oz (10 cups)

UK/Metric

Weight of yarn g (kg)	Dye solution required ml (l)
1g	5ml
10g	50ml
100g	500ml
1,000g (1kg)	5,000ml (5l)

You needn't use up all of the dyes you make up at the same time: fibre-reactive dyes will keep for a reasonable time if stored in a cool, dry place out of direct light and can therefore be used up at a later date. Make sure your dye solutions are labelled and dated and you can then use them for a future project. Be aware, however, that the dyes will lose strength over time so if you plan to use old dyes with new, you may not get the same depth of colour from an otherwise identical solution. As a guide, dyes will retain full strength for about one month, decreasing progressively thereafter.

A note on measurements
I have used US imperial and UK metric measurements throughout the book. However, my conversions are approximate and liberally rounded to permit easy measurement with basic equipment. Providing you are consistent in using US imperial, UK metric (or Canadian/Australian metric) you will achieve the right result.

Appendix F

Conversion charts

Crochet hook sizes			Knitting needle sizes		
USA	**UK**		**USA**	**UK metric**	**Old UK**
14 steel	0.60mm		0	2.00mm	14
12 steel	0.75mm		1	2.25mm	13
10 steel	1.00mm			2.50mm	
8 steel	1.25mm		2	2.75mm	12
7 steel	1.50mm			3.00mm	11
4 steel	1.75mm		3	3.25mm	10
0	2.00mm		4	3.50mm	
B	2.50mm		5	3.75mm	9
C	3.00mm		6	4.00mm	8
E	3.50mm		7	4.50mm	7
F	4.00mm		8	5.00mm	6
G	4.50mm		9	5.50mm	5
H	5.00mm		10	6.00mm	4
I	5.50mm		10$^{1}/_{2}$	6.50mm	3
J	6.00mm			7.00mm	2
K	7.00mm			7.50mm	1
11 wood	8.00mm		11	8.00mm	0
13 wood	9.00mm		13	9.00mm	00
15 wood	10.00mm		15	10.00mm	000
			17	12.75mm	

Fluid			Weight	
USA	**UK metric**		**USA**	**UK metric**
1tsp	5ml		1tsp	5g
1 fl oz	30ml		1oz	30g
1 cup	240ml*		1lb	480g
1gal	3.8l			

Length	
USA	**UK metric**
1in	2.5cm
1 yard	90cm

* Note: 250ml is used for metric dyes percentages for ease of conversion.

Appendix G

Commonly used US terms and their UK equivalents

I have written this book using mainly US terms. Below are listed some of the UK terms used in the book which may be described differently in the US and, in some cases, on the continent:

US Term	UK Equivalent
Slip stitch	Slip stitch
Single crochet	Double crochet
Half double crochet	Half treble crochet
Double crochet	Treble crochet
Treble crochet	Double treble crochet
Double treble crochet	Triple treble crochet
Yarn over hook	Wool round hook
Bind off	Cast off
Stockinette stitch	Stocking stitch
Gauge	Tension

Appendix H

Yarn thickness/weight conversions, suggested needle sizes and tension (gauge)

Listed below are a range of yarns and how they are described in various countries. A range of needle sizes and the approximate tension for each type of yarn is also included based on a 4in (10cm) square worked in stocking stitch. These are, of course, only a guide, but are useful as a general comparison if you are looking to substitute a different yarn from that given in a particular pattern.

US	Australia/NZ	UK	Suggested needle size	Approx. stitches over 4in (10cm) worked in stocking stitch
Light fingering		2ply	0–3 US 2–3.25mm	32–34
Fingering		3ply	3–5 US 3–3.75mm	26–31
Fingering/baby/sport	5ply	4ply	3–5 US 3–3.75mm	23–27
Sport/light worsted/knitting worsted/5ply	8ply	Double knitting (DK)	5–7 US 3.75–4.5mm	20–24
Aran/Heavy worsted	12ply	Aran	8–10 US 5–6mm	15–20
Bulky	14ply	Chunky	10–11 US 6–8mm	10–14
Super bulky		Super chunky	11–15 US 8–10mm	5–10

About the Author

Debbie Tomkies first became interested in crafts at the age of seven, when her gran taught her to knit. Her interest in knitting grew and led to spinning, and then to dyeing, when she wanted to use more exciting yarns and colours. She remains a keen spinner, and enjoys dyeing fleece and other fibres, as well as needlework and designing tapestry projects.

Debbie studied Greek and Latin at university and classics and classical art often inspire her work. She is a longstanding member of her local Guild of Spinners, Weavers & Dyers, and spent five years as treasurer of that Guild. She holds the City & Guilds certificate in preparing working designs, but acquired most of her skills informally, having been fortunate in meeting a large number of talented teachers and craftspeople who have willingly shared their knowledge and enthusiasm.

Debbie is married to Peter Tomkies, who provided the step-by-step photographs and colour diagrams for this book, and they have a nine-year-old son, William.

Index

TITLES AVAILABLE FROM
GMC Publications

BOOKS

WOODCARVING

Beginning Woodcarving	GMC Publications
Carving Architectural Detail in Wood: The Classical Tradition	Frederick Wilbur
Carving Birds & Beasts	GMC Publications
Carving Classical Styles in Wood	Frederick Wilbur
Carving the Human Figure: Studies in Wood and Stone	Dick Onians
Carving Nature: Wildlife Studies in Wood	Frank Fox-Wilson
Celtic Carved Lovespoons: 30 Patterns	Sharon Littley & Clive Griffin
Decorative Woodcarving (New Edition)	Jeremy Williams
Elements of Woodcarving	Chris Pye
Figure Carving in Wood: Human and Animal Forms	Sara Wilkinson
Lettercarving in Wood: A Practical Course	Chris Pye
Relief Carving in Wood: A Practical Introduction	Chris Pye
Woodcarving for Beginners	GMC Publications
Woodcarving Made Easy	Cynthia Rogers
Woodcarving Tools, Materials & Equipment (New Edition in 2 vols.)	Chris Pye

WOODTURNING

Bowl Turning Techniques Masterclass	Tony Boase
Chris Child's Projects for Woodturners	Chris Child
Decorating Turned Wood: The Maker's Eye	Liz & Michael O'Donnell
Green Woodwork	Mike Abbott
A Guide to Work-Holding on the Lathe	Fred Holder
Keith Rowley's Woodturning Projects	Keith Rowley
Making Screw Threads in Wood	Fred Holder
Segmented Turning: A Complete Guide	Ron Hampton
Turned Boxes: 50 Designs	Chris Stott
Turning Green Wood	Michael O'Donnell
Turning Pens and Pencils	Kip Christensen & Rex Burningham
Wood for Woodturners	Mark Baker
Woodturning: Forms and Materials	John Hunnex
Woodturning: A Foundation Course (New Edition)	Keith Rowley
Woodturning: A Fresh Approach	Robert Chapman
Woodturning: An Individual Approach	Dave Regester
Woodturning: A Source Book of Shapes	John Hunnex
Woodturning Masterclass	Tony Boase
Woodturning Projects: A Workshop Guide to Shapes	Mark Baker

WOODWORKING

Beginning Picture Marquetry	Lawrence Threadgold
Carcass Furniture	GMC Publications
Celtic Carved Lovespoons: 30 Patterns	Sharon Littley & Clive Griffin
Celtic Woodcraft	Glenda Bennett
Celtic Woodworking Projects	Glenda Bennett
Complete Woodfinishing (Revised Edition)	Ian Hosker
David Charlesworth's Furniture-Making Techniques	David Charlesworth
David Charlesworth's Furniture-Making Techniques – Volume 2	David Charlesworth
Furniture Projects with the Router	Kevin Ley
Furniture Restoration (Practical Crafts)	Kevin Jan Bonner
Furniture Restoration: A Professional at Work	John Lloyd
Furniture Workshop	Kevin Ley

Green Woodwork	Mike Abbott
History of Furniture: Ancient to 1900	Michael Huntley
Intarsia: 30 Patterns for the Scrollsaw	John Everett
Making Heirloom Boxes	Peter Lloyd
Making Screw Threads in Wood	Fred Holder
Making Woodwork Aids and Devices	Robert Wearing
Mastering the Router	Ron Fox
Pine Furniture Projects for the Home	Dave Mackenzie
Router Magic: Jigs, Fixtures and Tricks to Unleash your Router's Full Potential	Bill Hylton
Router Projects for the Home	GMC Publications
Router Tips & Techniques	Robert Wearing
Routing: A Workshop Handbook	Anthony Bailey
Routing for Beginners (Revised and Expanded Edition)	Anthony Bailey
Stickmaking: A Complete Course	Andrew Jones & Clive George
Stickmaking Handbook	Andrew Jones & Clive George
Storage Projects for the Router	GMC Publications
Success with Sharpening	Ralph Laughton
Veneering: A Complete Course	Ian Hosker
Veneering Handbook	Ian Hosker
Wood: Identification & Use	Terry Porter
Woodworking Techniques and Projects	Anthony Bailey
Woodworking with the Router: Professional Router Techniques any Woodworker can Use	Bill Hylton & Fred Matlack

UPHOLSTERY

Upholstery: A Beginners' Guide	David James
Upholstery: A Complete Course (Revised Edition)	David James
Upholstery Restoration	David James
Upholstery Techniques & Projects	David James
Upholstery Tips and Hints	David James

DOLLS' HOUSES AND MINIATURES

1/12 Scale Character Figures for the Dolls' House	James Carrington
Americana in 1/12 Scale: 50 Authentic Projects	Joanne Ogreenc & Mary Lou Santovec
The Authentic Georgian Dolls' House	Brian Long
A Beginners' Guide to the Dolls' House Hobby	Jean Nisbett
Celtic, Medieval and Tudor Wall Hangings in 1/12 Scale Needlepoint	Sandra Whitehead
Creating Decorative Fabrics: Projects in 1/12 Scale	Janet Storey
Dolls' House Accessories, Fixtures and Fittings	Andrea Barham
Dolls' House Furniture: Easy-to-Make Projects in 1/12 Scale	Freida Gray
Dolls' House Makeovers	Jean Nisbett
Dolls' House Window Treatments	Eve Harwood
Edwardian-Style Hand-Knitted Fashion for 1/12 Scale Dolls	Yvonne Wakefield
How to Make Your Dolls' House Special: Fresh Ideas for Decorating	Beryl Armstrong
Making 1/12 Scale Wicker Furniture for the Dolls' House	Sheila Smith
Making Miniature Chinese Rugs and Carpets	Carol Phillipson
Making Miniature Food and Market Stalls	Angie Scarr

CRAFTS

GARDENING

PHOTOGRAPHY

ART TECHNIQUES

VIDEOS

MAGAZINES

WOODTURNING ◆ WOODCARVING ◆ FURNITURE & CABINETMAKING
THE ROUTER ◆ NEW WOODWORKING ◆ THE DOLLS' HOUSE MAGAZINE
OUTDOOR PHOTOGRAPHY ◆ BLACK & WHITE PHOTOGRAPHY
KNITTING ◆ GUILD NEWS

The above represents a full list of all titles currently published or scheduled to be published.
All are available direct from the Publishers or through bookshops, newsagents and specialist retailers.
To place an order, or to obtain a complete catalogue, contact:

GMC Publications,
Castle Place, 166 High Street, Lewes, East Sussex BN7 1XU United Kingdom
Tel: 01273 488005 Fax: 01273 402866
E-mail: pubs@thegmcgroup.com
Website: www.gmcbooks.com

Orders by credit card are accepted